A FULL-LENGTH PLAY

Here and Now

by

DAVID ROGERS

THE DRAMATIC PUBLISHING COMPANY
311 Washington Street, P.O. Box 109
Woodstock, Illinois 60098

MIDDLEBURY COLLEGE LIBRARY

*** NOTICE ***

The amateur and stock acting rights to this work are controlled exclusively by THE DRAMATIC PUBLISHING COMPANY without whose permission in writing no performance of it may be given. Royalty fees are given in our current catalogue and are subject to change without notice. Royalty must be paid every time a play is performed whether it is prested for charity or for profit and whether or not admission is charged. A play is performed anytime it is acted before an audience. All inquiries concerning amateur and stock rights should be addressed to: THE DRAMATIC PUBLISHING COMPANY, P. O. Box 109, Woodstock, Illinois 60098.

COPYRIGHT LAW GIVES THE AUTHOR OR HIS AGENT
THE EXCLUSIVE RIGHT TO MAKE COPIES.

This law provides authors with a fair return for their creative efforts. Authors earn their living from the royalties they receive from book sales and from the performance of their work. Conscientious observance of copyright law is not only ethical, it encourages authors to continue their creative work.

HERE AND NOW

is fully protected by copyright. No alterations, deletions or substitutions may be made in the work without the prior written consent of the publisher. No part of this work may be reproduced or transmitted in any form or by any means, electronic or mechanical, including photocopy, recording, videotape, film, or any information storage and retrieval system, without permission in writing from the publisher. It may not be performed either by professionals or amateurs without payment of royalty. All rights, including but not limited to the professional, motion picture, radio, television, videotape, foreign language, tabloid, recitation, lecturing, publication, and reading are reserved. On all programs this notice should appear: Produced by special arrangement with THE DRAMATIC PUBLISHING COMPANY of Woodstock, Illinois.

©MCMLXXIII by
DAVID ROGERS
Printed in the United States of America
All Rights Reserved
(HERE AND NOW)

HERE AND NOW

A Full-Length Play

For Six Men, Seven Women and Three Parts
That May Be Either

CHARACTERS

See Author's Note on Characters, page 5 and 6.

PLACE: *The stage of the high school.*

TIME: *The present.*

The material of the play within the play "Here and Now" has been suggested by the work of Robert Selverstone, Ph. D., Director of Human Relations for the Westport, Connecticut Public Schools. While the events in the play are entirely fictitious and the techniques not necessarily those employed by Dr. Selverstone and any resemblance of the characters to any persons living or dead is purely coincidental, the author would like to express his deep appreciation to Dr. Selverstone for his help, guidance and criticism in creating the events and characters portrayed.

AUTHOR'S NOTE

"Here and Now" is an unusual play and requires some unusual devices to achieve its maximum effect. It is, actually, a play within a play, and to heighten the theatricality of the play within the play the outside material must be done very realistically. Therefore, I have suggested that the actors in the play appear as themselves, using their own real names. For purposes of printing simplification, I have titled the speeches in their own person, Actor Who Plays Paul or Actress Who Plays Jane, etc. Further, to make for easier reading, I have called the stage managers Elaine and Marvin, but I would prefer the actors playing these roles to use their own names, too. If more convenient, both roles could be played by men or women. Also, Mr. Harris, the director, could be Miss Harris. Another interesting possibility might be to have the actual director of the play assume this part under his or her own name.

Other minor changes to make this specifically your group, your school, are encouraged. I have referred to the Drama Group as "Dram Soc" but if yours is called "The Thespians" or "The Players," please change the name to conform. The same holds true of the ticket price or any other specific.

I suggest that the names of the actors be printed in the program without any character designation, and that the scenes be listed in this manner:

SCENE ONE:	The first rehearsal.
SCENE TWO:	The second week of rehearsal.
SCENE THREE:	The third week of rehearsal.
SCENE FOUR:	Dress rehearsal.
SCENES FIVE, SIX, SEVEN and EIGHT:	Tonight. The performance.

I further suggest that, although the play will be performed with an intermission, as a trick to fool the audience into further believing the reality of the situation, you print in the program the line: "The play will be performed without an intermission."

I think the above will prepare the audience for an unusual evening even before the play begins.

David Rogers

Scene 1

(When the audience enters the auditorium, the stage
    curtain is up but the stage unlit. The stage
    looks exactly as it would on any day when
    the auditorium is not in use. There are a
    few nondescript-looking chairs, a stool
    and a piano bench scattered about.

About five minutes before the play is sched-
    uled to begin, ELAINE and MARVIN, the
    stage manager and her assistant, come on
    stage carrying a small table which they set
    DR. ELAINE goes off and gets a chair
    which she brings on and places downstage
    of the table. She then joins MARVIN in
    moving the chairs, stool and piano bench
    into a rough semi-circle downstage, leaving
    a playing area in front of them. Neither of
    them, nor the other actors who will soon
    enter, pay any attention to the audience,
    which may or may not react to them. As
    far as they are all concerned, the audito-
    rium is empty.

After about two minutes, the ACTOR WHO
    PLAYS STU comes on from the wings,
    greets them quietly and helps them move
    chairs. A minute later the ACTOR WHO
    PLAYS JERRY and the ACTRESS WHO
    PLAYS KIM enter together.)

ACTOR WHO PLAYS JERRY (to others). Hi . . .
ACTRESS WHO PLAYS KIM. The first rehearsal!
    Isn't this exciting?

MARVIN (not impressed).   Eh . . .

(ACTOR WHO PLAYS SHEB enters from the wings.)

ACTOR WHO PLAYS SHEB (to ELAINE).   Can't we
          have the lights on?
ELAINE (embarrassed).   I couldn't find the switch.
ACTOR WHO PLAYS SHEB.   Some stage manager!
          It's like rehearsing in the Haunted House at
          Disneyland.
ACTOR WHO PLAYS JERRY.   I'll show you where
          it is.

(He goes off R with ELAINE as the ACTRESSES WHO
          PLAY VICKIE and JANE enter down the
          aisle.)

ACTRESS WHO PLAYS JANE (calling from aisle).
          Hello . . .
ACTRESS WHO PLAYS VICKIE (from the aisle).
          Are we late?
ACTOR WHO PLAYS STU (calling back).   No. Mr.
          Harris isn't here yet.

(The girls go up on stage as ACTORS WHO PLAY
          PAUL and DON enter L.)

ACTOR WHO PLAYS PAUL.   Can't start without the
          director.

(The stage lights go on just as the ACTRESS WHO
          PLAYS BARBARA enters L.   Taking ad-
          vantage of the lights, kidding, she sweeps
          across downstage, fake gracious-dramatic.)

ACTRESS WHO PLAYS BARBARA.   I want to thank
          you all for giving me this Academy Award

and I just want to say there is absolutely no
one I have to thank. I did it all myself.
(The others laugh. The house lights go off.)
ACTOR WHO PLAYS SHEB. I think you blew a
fuse.

(ACTRESS WHO PLAYS DODIE has come halfway
down the aisle, in the dark.)

ACTRESS WHO PLAYS DODIE. Don't turn out the
lights . . . a person could kill herself in
the dark!
ACTRESS WHO PLAYS JANE (calling to her). That's
show business,_____(She uses Actress Who
Plays Dodie's real name.)

(ELAINE and ACTOR WHO PLAYS JERRY return R.
He moves to ACTRESS WHO PLAYS VICKIE
as ACTRESS WHO PLAYS DODIE comes up
on stage.)

ACTRESS WHO PLAYS KIM (to ACTOR WHO PLAYS
JERRY). It is exciting! (Looking out front.)
Just being in a theatre . . . even when it's
empty . . . and standing on a stage . . . it
doesn't matter if there's scenery or lights
. . . there's a feeling that something's
going to happen . . . you're going to learn
or be moved or somehow become more
than you are . . .
ACTOR WHO PLAYS DON. This stuff really turns
you on? You want to be an actress or
something?
ACTOR WHO PLAYS JERRY (defending her). Why
not?
ACTRESS WHO PLAYS DODIE. It's better than
working in the five and ten.

ACTRESS WHO PLAYS BARBARA. It could be
         very glamorous.
ACTRESS WHO PLAYS KIM. It's not the glamour!
         It's communicating with people . . . on a
         deeper level than you do when you just talk.
         That's what theatre means. And this play
         . . . "Here and Now" . . . I think it's going
         to be very exciting to work on.
ACTRESS WHO PLAYS JANE. Maybe too exciting.
ACTOR WHO PLAYS JERRY. Now, don't start that
         again,_____ .

(He uses her real name but breaks off as MR.
         HARRIS, the director, enters L carrying
         a brief case.)

HARRIS (moving across stage to table DR). OK.
         OK. Time to go to work. (Others break
         from their positions at the start of what was
         about to be an argument. They ad lib
         greetings: "Hi" . . . "Hello, Mr. Harris"
         . . . "We're ready" . . . etc. HARRIS
         puts his brief case on table and opens it.)
         Is everybody here?

(ACTRESS WHO PLAYS CLAIRE has entered and
         started up the aisle.)

ACTRESS WHO PLAYS CLAIRE (somewhere in the
         aisle, guilty at almost being late). I'm
         here . . . I'm here . . . I'll be right there
         . . . I'm here . . . (She comes up on
         stage.) I did this dumb thing . . . I was
         thinking today was Tuesday and I got half
         way home before I . . . (Realizing she's
         talking too much.) I'm here.
HARRIS. Fine. (He takes playbooks out of his brief

case and begins to distribute them from
stage R to L.) You all know which parts
you're playing. . . . Please be careful
with the books; I don't want to have to
send for more. . . .

(As he reaches L, ACTRESS WHO PLAYS ADELE
enters L and he hands her a copy.)

ACTRESS WHO PLAYS ADELE. Mr. Harris, my
mother said I should tell you that she
doesn't approve of this play.
HARRIS. Has she read it?
ACTRESS WHO PLAYS ADELE. No. But I told her
about it. And she wanted you to know.
HARRIS. All right. I know. (He returns to his
table, sits, opens a notebook.)
ACTRESS WHO PLAYS ADELE (to the others). Are
you sure you don't want to change your mind?
I mean, it's not too late to do another play.
ACTRESS WHO PLAYS VICKIE. Oh, come on,
_____(She uses Actress Who Plays Adele's
real name.) The Dram Soc voted democrat-
ically and this play won.
ACTRESS WHO PLAYS DODIE. Only by two votes!
ACTOR WHO PLAYS JERRY. I thought you liked this
play!
ACTRESS WHO PLAYS DODIE. I do. I love it.
I think it's fascinating.
ACTRESS WHO PLAYS JANE. I just don't know if
it's right for a high school group.
ACTRESS WHO PLAYS DODIE (agreeing with her).
It is a little strong.
ACTOR WHO PLAYS SHEB. Whose side are you on?
ACTRESS WHO PLAYS DODIE (anxious to please).
Nobody's. I think you're both right.

(ACTOR WHO PLAYS TONY is coming down the
        aisle.)

ACTOR WHO PLAYS TONY (forcefully, using Actress
        Who Plays Jane's real name)_____is right.
        We can't do this play. We'll have to pick
        something else. (HARRIS looks up, listens.
        The next speeches are spoken simultaneously.)
ACTRESS WHO PLAYS VICKIE. Why shouldn't we
        do it?
ACTRESS WHO PLAYS BARBARA. Who are you to
        say what we should or shouldn't do?
ACTRESS WHO PLAYS KIM. This is the best play
        we've had in years.
ACTOR WHO PLAYS DON. Do we have to start
        this again?
ACTRESS WHO PLAYS DODIE. I hate it when
        people change their minds.
ACTRESS WHO PLAYS JANE. You're absolutely
        right. We can't do it.
ACTOR WHO PLAYS PAUL. It's got a lot of good
        things in it.
ACTRESS WHO PLAYS ADELE. And a lot of things
        I don't want to say . . . (By now ACTOR
        WHO PLAYS TONY is on stage.)
HARRIS. Wait a minute, everybody. I thought we
        settled all this.
ACTOR WHO PLAYS TONY. Yes, we did . . . but
        I've been thinking and thinking . . . and look,
        this play . . . well, it cuts too deep. It's
        into things people get upset about.
ACTRESS WHO PLAYS BARBARA. That's exactly
        why we should do it! It's a play about a
        human relations group where high school
        students and teachers and parents meet and
        talk about their feelings . . . try to resolve

their problems. It deals with real problems.
ACTOR WHO PLAYS JERRY. Why can't we for
        once do a play that has some depth?
ACTRESS WHO PLAYS JANE. 'Cause it's safer to
        do one that has some shallow.
ACTRESS WHO PLAYS ADELE. Imagine talking
        about . . . personal problems. With parents!
        It's pure science fiction.
ACTOR WHO PLAYS PAUL. It's real. There are
        groups like this. They've been tried a lot
        of places . . . and very successfully.
ACTOR WHO PLAYS TONY. Maybe you can discuss
        intimate things like this in a . . . a kind of
        encounter group atmosphere . . . but you
        can't talk about them on a stage.
ACTRESS WHO PLAYS ADELE. My mother says
        there are some things ladies don't talk
        about anywhere.
ACTOR WHO PLAYS SHEB. We talk about them.
        In the cafeteria . . . the halls. . . . Why
        not on stage?
ACTRESS WHO PLAYS JANE. 'Cause there'll be
        people listening!
ACTOR WHO PLAYS SHEB. I'm not talking to my-
        self in the cafeteria. Not yet, anyway.
ACTRESS WHO PLAYS ADELE. She means an
        audience . . . a large group of heaven
        knows who.
ACTOR WHO PLAYS JERRY. As business manager
        of the club, I certainly hope it'll be large.
ACTRESS WHO PLAYS CLAIRE. Please don't make
        another speech about selling tickets.
HARRIS. We're wasting a lot of time. We discussed
        this play and the other choices weeks ago . . .
        everybody had a chance to speak then. There
        was a vote and "Here and Now" won.

ACTOR WHO PLAYS PAUL. And that should settle
          it.

HARRIS. Frankly, I was surprised by your choice
          . . . but very pleased. I think it's time
          we did a play that has meaning for all of us.

ACTOR WHO PLAYS TONY (tense). But suppose this
          play really gets to somebody? Suppose you
          hit a nerve too hard and some kid flakes
          out watching this?

HARRIS. Maybe that could happen. There are lots
          of people that are up tight about these
          situations . . . but maybe they won't flake
          out . . . maybe they'll learn something.
          Maybe it'll help them.

ACTOR WHO PLAYS TONY. And maybe it'll do
          something real bad to them.

HARRIS. I'd be sorry if you felt you couldn't be in the
          play,_____--(He uses Actor Who Plays Tony's
          real name.)--but if you want out, I under-
          stand. (ACTOR WHO PLAYS TONY stands,
          torn, trying to decide.)

ACTOR WHO PLAYS JERRY. You seem pretty
          tense about all this. Are you afraid you'll
          flake out?

ACTOR WHO PLAYS TONY (defensive). No!

ACTOR WHO PLAYS JERRY. Then?

ACTOR WHO PLAYS TONY. I'm not quitting.

HARRIS. Anybody else who'd rather not be in it?
          (He looks at ACTRESS WHO PLAYS ADELE.
          She turns away. He looks at ACTRESS
          WHO PLAYS JANE, uses her real name.)
          . . . ?

ACTRESS WHO PLAYS JANE (angrily). I like being
          in plays. Even plays I don't like!

HARRIS. All right, then. Let's rehearse. Will
          everyone sit down, please? (The actors

all take chairs. Stage managers each go
to one side of the stage.)

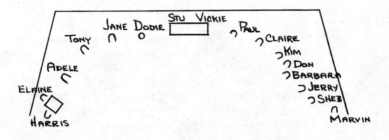

(The setting is the empty stage of a high school audi-
        torium.)

ACTOR WHO PLAYS SHEB. Are you sure we can
        do it on our scenery budget?
ACTRESS WHO PLAYS JANE (a further grievance).
        And there are no costumes!
HARRIS. Just the sort of things you'd wear to any
        meeting. Maybe those of you who are playing
        adults . . . that's Adele, Claire, Paul,
        Stu and Barbara . . . I think you can be a
        little better dressed than the kids.
ACTRESS WHO PLAYS KIM. That is over-30
        chauvinism. I dress as well as any of the
        old folks I know.
ACTRESS WHO PLAYS ADELE. See? It's beginning
        to upset us already.
HARRIS. No. I shouldn't have said that. It's already
        helping me to understand better. Now, when
        the play begins, you're sitting right where
        you are now.
ACTOR WHO PLAYS DON. Like this?
HARRIS. Right. Mark it, Elaine. (She makes note

⸴   in her script.) You're a casual group of
          strangers who have come together for a
          meeting. Just you, Tony . . . change
          seats with Sheb. Tony always sits alone
          on the side . . . afraid to be involved.

ACTOR WHO PLAYS TONY (as they change seats).
          I don't blame him.

HARRIS. Let's just read through the script today
          and see how we feel about the parts we're
          playing. If you have any questions about
          your characterizations, I'll try to answer
          them.

ACTRESS WHO PLAYS DODIE. I start by clearing
          my throat?

HARRIS. Give it some time first. Curtain goes up
          on absolute silence. I want the audience to
          feel you've been there for minutes saying
          nothing. It's the first group meeting. You
          all feel uncomfortable. Strange. Take as
          much time as you like. Curtain.

(As the actors begin the scene from the play within
          the play, they seem actually to read the
          lines, but within a page or so, blend
          away from staring constantly into the books,
          which would be dull for the audience.
          Glance at them and look up to say the lines
          . . . make it a stage convention that you
          are reading rather than actually doing so.
          When speaking as the actors, hold the
          books down in a definite way so the audi-
          ence knows when you are the part and
          when you are the actor.

          They all sit, staring straight ahead. After
          a beat, DODIE clears her throat. They all
          look at her.)

DODIE (smiling, sheepishly). Nothing . . . (Another
        beat.)
ACTOR WHO PLAYS STU (to HARRIS). It says I take
        out a pack of cigarettes--(HARRIS nods.)--
        then I say . . . (As character.) May I smoke?
BARBARA. Cigarettes?
STU. What else?
BARBARA. I don't think it's allowed in the auditorium.
SHEB. But in the men's room . . . anything goes!
ACTOR WHO PLAYS STU. It says I glare at him and
        rise impatiently.
HARRIS. Yes. Get up and walk over right. . . .
ACTRESS WHO PLAYS CLAIRE. Shall I go on?
HARRIS. Please.
CLAIRE (to PAUL). Why are we in the auditorium?
        It seems like a strange place for this kind
        of meeting.
PAUL.   Some of the teachers didn't want us in the
        teachers' lounge, there's some kind of team
        practice in the gym, which means the cafeteria
        would be too noisy, and Thursday nights the
        Spanish society meets in the library.
ADELE. There must be fifty or sixty classrooms.
PAUL. The custodian says that interferes with his
        cleaning.
SHEB. Very interesting . . . but stupid! The
        principal thinks he's running this high
        school, the school board thinks they're
        running it, but when you come right down
        to the nitty gritty, it's the janitor tells
        you what you can do. (A beat. JANE rises
        and moves to Stu's former chair beside
        VICKIE.)
JANE. May I sit next to you?
VICKIE. Why . . . sure.
JANE. I met you at the orchestra try-out? . . . I
        played the Brahms?

VICKIE. Oh, yes. You were marvelous. (JANE
    sits beside her.)

STU (irritable). Is this all we're going to do? Just
    look at each other for two hours?

PAUL. You can do anything you want. Talk about
    anything that concerns you.

STU. Well, aren't you going to start us off? You're
    the group leader. The therapist.

PAUL. No. I'm not a therapist . . . and you're not
    patients.

KIM. Then what are we here for?

VICKIE. Talk.

SHEB (singing). "Getting to know you . . ."

PAUL. Exactly. We are a group of healthy people . . .

KIM. Ha!

PAUL. Presumably. (He rises, walks as he talks.)
    The idea is to break down the stereotype
    reactions we have to each other as parents
    . . . teachers . . . pupils. It's called a
    Here and Now group because we're supposed
    to discuss what's bothering us here and now.
    If we let it all hang out, maybe we'll be
    a little less uptight . . . understand each
    other . . . and ourselves . . . a little
    better. (He winds up DL.)

ADELE. Well, how does it work? Do we all take
    turns with our neuroses?

PAUL. No. Anyone can say anything. Any time.
    The only rules are: no smoking, no fist
    fights and nothing that happens here can
    be talked about outside the group.

CLAIRE (doubtfully). Well, I suppose that's all
    right . . . as long as there are parents
    here.

KIM (putting CLAIRE on, fake Southern accent).
    Lawsy, lawsy! Ah don't go nowhere without
    mah chaperone!

DON. You're being rude.

KIM (looking at him, slightly patronizing). Oh, yes.
        You're that football one. I can tell by your
        cast.

ACTOR WHO PLAYS DON (to HARRIS). What does
        that mean? About the cast?

HARRIS. Don's wearing one. He has a broken hand.

ACTRESS WHO PLAYS BARBARA. I'm glad I'm
        not doing props for this show.

HARRIS. As the play progresses, your cast comes
        off. It shows the passage of time. They
        have eight sessions . . . eight weeks . . .
        eight scenes in the play. Take it from Kim's
        line.

KIM. Oh, yes. You're that football one. I can tell
        by your cast.

DON (reserved, not liking the girl or her tone). I'm
        on the team.

KIM (putting him on). Don't put yourself down. You
        are the team. The guy with a pigskin heart.
        Broke the hand in a pileup last Saturday and
        played the last seven minutes in agony,
        winning the hearts of all with your bravery
        even though we lost. (Mock innocent.)
        Didn't it hurt?

DON. Yes.

STU (moving to him). Are you that kid? (Impressed.)
        I read about that.

KIM (to DON). What's a nice jock like you doing in
        a place like this?

ACTOR WHO PLAYS DON (to HARRIS). It says I
        walk away here.

HARRIS. Yes. You don't like her. Go over left.
        (DON walks R.) Left.

ACTOR WHO PLAYS DON. This is left.

HARRIS. Not the audience's left. Your left.

ACTOR WHO PLAYS DON. I don't know if I can do

this. I've never been in a play before.

HARRIS. You'll be fine. All you have to learn is
which is your left side.

ACTOR WHO PLAYS SHEB. The hand with the
watch on it.

ACTRESS WHO PLAYS KIM. I don't understand
those lines. Does Kim like him or not?

HARRIS. What do you think?

ACTRESS WHO PLAYS KIM. I don't know.

ACTRESS WHO PLAYS VICKIE. I think she likes
him but either she doesn't want to show it
. . . or she's the kind of girl who . . .
y'know . . . works against herself when
she wants something.

ACTRESS WHO PLAYS KIM. What do I do? Pick
one from Column A?

HARRIS. Just go on. It'll all come clear as you
work on it. Stu . . .

ACTOR WHO PLAYS STU (finding place in script).
She says "what's a nice jock . . ." and so on
. . . (To KIM, in character.) You could
learn a little from him, young lady. If
there were more kids like him in this town
. . . kids that care . . . this'd be a
better place to live.

JERRY. Yeah, but what's he care about? Football.
What's so great about that? If those eleven
guys would use their heads for thinking instead
of for butting another eleven guys around
in the mud, then she could learn from
him. (To HARRIS, as himself.) Why am I
saying that?

HARRIS. Well, Jerry is defensive. . . .

ACTOR WHO PLAYS JERRY. About what?

HARRIS. He's a brain . . . not very muscular.

ACTOR WHO PLAYS JERRY. You should've got a
97-pound weakling for this part.

OK. I'm defensive. (He makes a note in
his playbook.) Go right ahead. I don't
say anything for pages.

HARRIS. All right, another pause . . . then, Dodie,
you take out a chocolate bar and take a bite.

ACTRESS WHO PLAYS DODIE. I don't have enough
trouble, you give me a part where the
girl is always eating.

HARRIS. Stu's line. . . . Go to him, Stu.

STU (walking to PAUL, DL). Look, Mr. Tobin . . .

PAUL. Paul.

STU. OK, Paul. I got talked into this clambake. I
don't really think this kind of thing does anybody any good, but if all we're going to do is
sit here and listen to smart remarks, I
brought a lot of work home from the
office . . .

VICKIE (hastily). Why don't we just introduce
ourselves to start?

CLAIRE. But don't you children know each other
already?

SHEB. This is a very big high school. We don't all
have our milk and cookies together.

STU. That's just the kind of thing I mean.

PAUL (to CLAIRE). We try to make sure students
and teachers in our groups don't know each
other. And we never allow parents in a
group with their own children.

KIM. I guess that brings down the level of violence.

STU. Thank you and good night. (He starts out L.)

ADELE. Why don't you give it a chance? (He
hesitates.) Please. (STU returns and sits
in Don's former chair.)

DODIE. Why don't we tell why we joined the group,
too?

PAUL. Tell what you want. Why did you? (He sits
right of DODIE.)

DODIE. I thought it would be very informative. How
　　　　people think and all. . . . My name is Dodie
　　　　Rydell.
SHEB (rising). My name is Shelby Morton but you can
　　　　call me Sheb. I joined because--(Portentously.)
　　　　--It is the only school-supervised activity I
　　　　know--(Changing his tone.)--where you can
　　　　do it and lie down at the same time. (He
　　　　lies down on the floor.)
VICKIE. I'm Vickie Sloper. I'm a junior. I was
　　　　in an encounter group that my church spon-
　　　　sored last summer. I found it very inter-
　　　　esting. I learned about myself . . . a little.
　　　　I thought maybe I'd learn some more.
DODIE (to DON). I wonder why a great football hero
　　　　like you would join a group like this?
DON (coming down to chair left of VICKIE). Why not?
　　　　The coach won't let me play. (As himself.)
　　　　Then I show my hand in the cast, I guess
　　　　. . . (As DON.) What else have I got to
　　　　do? (He sits.) My name is Don Coyle.
　　　　I'm a senior.
KIM. But anyone who reads the sports page knows
　　　　that.
DON. What are you doing here?
KIM. I dig trying everything. At least once. Kim
　　　　Lockwood.
DODIE (to PAUL). Do you take a turn? Or are you
　　　　just above us all?
PAUL. I'm part of the group. But you know who I
　　　　am and why I'm here.
STU (moving to PAUL). I don't. You're here and it's
　　　　costing the school board a lot of money just
　　　　for twelve people to understand each other.
JERRY. Why does understanding threaten you?
PAUL. It's not just these twelve people. If this
　　　　pilot group works, there'll be a lot more

groups. And then maybe the kids around here and the parents will be better able to cope with the pressures and the problems.

KIM. We'll all be so secure, we'll give up mouth-wash.

STU. My daughter hassled me into coming here. But after a long day at the office, I don't really need all this psychological . . . hog-wash.

JERRY (the super-psychiatrist). Why did you really say that?

STU (annoyed). 'Cause that's what I meant!

JERRY (wisely). I wonder. . . .

ACTRESS WHO PLAYS ADELE (reading stage direction). Adele, trying to change the subject . . . (As character.) Why don't you tell us your name?

STU. Stu Ainsley. I don't think I'll be back. (Looking at PAUL, a put down.) And what kind of problems do high school kids have anyway? (JERRY laughs at him. STU looks at JERRY.)

SHEB (rising to sitting position). I didn't think that kind existed any more. (STU glares at him. SHEB pantomimes being shot in the heart.) Oooh. He got me. (He falls back to the floor. STU walks upstage and stands looking at back wall.)

ADELE. I think, as parents, we could learn a lot here. I'm Adele Chapman.

CLAIRE (nodding wisely). It's a mother's duty to understand.

KIM. Tell me that's for real.

BARBARA. I'm Barbara Ekstrom. I teach English. I want this group to work. I want this program to go on because there are problems in this school, Mr. Ainsley. In almost any school.

STU (turning). Talking never solved any problems.

JANE (bursting out). It might! I mean, if people talk,
        it's better than nothing. I'm sorry. I'm
        Jane Owens. I'm just a freshman.

CLAIRE. It's all right to be a freshman, darling. We
        all want to know what the freshmen are
        thinking. Feel free, Joan.

JANE (correcting her). Jane.

CLAIRE. Of course. My name is Mrs. Walter
        Newell.

JERRY. Do you want us to call you Mrs. Newell or
        Walter?

CLAIRE (glaring at him). The adults may call me
        Claire, if they wish, but I do believe that
        observing at least some of the proprieties,
        such as respect for elders, does make
        life more gracious, don't you? (She smiles
        at the whole group.)

KIM. You bet your bottom, Mrs. Walter. (CLAIRE
        looks shocked.)

STU (coming down to PAUL). Are you going to permit
        that?

PAUL. Kim's free to react. So are you. So is Claire.
        Have you anything to say?

CLAIRE (icy). I think not.

JERRY (to STU). What did you want him to do?
        Spank Kim?

STU (going to JERRY, standing over him, menacing).
        What is your name?

JERRY (rising). Jerry Martinez, Stu.

STU. And why did you join the group, Mr. Martinez?

JERRY. I thought I might find out why the older
        generation was so uptight. (They look
        almost about to fight.)

ADELE (pointing to TONY). We haven't heard from
        that boy. (They all look at TONY.) Not at all.

TONY. I'm Tony Baldwin. I . . . I just wanted to
          watch.
HARRIS. That's a blackout, Elaine.
ELAINE (rising). Yes. I know which switch that
          is. (She goes off R. Some of the actors
          rise, move about.)
HARRIS. That's not bad for a first reading. . . .
ACTRESS WHO PLAYS CLAIRE. I think it's going
          to be fascinating.
ACTRESS WHO PLAYS JANE. Why haven't we ever
          done "The Taming of the Shrew"?
HARRIS. Let's take a break and then read Scene
          Two.

                          BLACKOUT

Scene 2

(A week later. As lights come up, the stage is as it
          was. All the actors and MARVIN are in
          small groups, some seated, some standing,
          chatting, waiting for rehearsal to begin.
          HARRIS immediately enters L, moving to
          his table DR.)

HARRIS (talking as he comes). All right. I want to
          start tonight by reviewing Scene Two. (Con-
          versation stops. A few move to pick up
          their playbooks.)
ACTOR WHO PLAYS DON. Can we use our books?
HARRIS. Tonight, if necessary. But starting with
          the next rehearsal everyone is to have all
          their lines down. You should remember
          your moves but if you don't, Elaine will
          cue you.
MARVIN (crossing to him). Elaine won't be here
          tonight. She pulled a muscle in her back in
          school this morning.
ACTRESS WHO PLAYS DODIE. I always said those
          gym classes were too strenuous.
MARVIN. She wasn't in gym. She was taking a
          geometry test.
ACTOR WHO PLAYS TONY. How can you pull a
          muscle taking a geometry test?
MARVIN. How would I know? I take algebra.
HARRIS (to MARVIN). Well, I hope you marked the
          moves.
MARVIN. No. But I have her book.
HARRIS. Good.
MARVIN. I just can't read her writing.
HARRIS (giving up). Do you all remember where

26

you were at the beginning of Scene Two?
(The actors ad lib "Yes," "I was over
there," "I think so," etc. as they move
to their places.)

ACTOR WHO PLAYS DON. I was on the floor
over there . . . (He walks DR and stands.)

ACTRESS WHO PLAYS KIM. This is the one where
Dodie is talking and I pace up and down
over there. (She goes L.)

ACTRESS WHO PLAYS ADELE. No, you were pacing
on this side. Remember, you knocked over
my bottle of coke?

ACTRESS WHO PLAYS KIM (going R). I said I was
sorry.

HARRIS. Good. Don, on the floor--(DON sits.)--
and as the lights come up, Dodie, you're
talking.

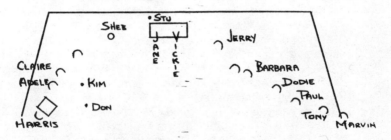

(ADELE, JERRY and KIM do not use books; others
carry them but refer to them only occasionally.
This is almost a smooth performance.)

DODIE. So there I was in this elevator . . .
MARVIN (sitting down L with script). Wait a minute!
HARRIS. What's wrong?
MARVIN. I didn't say "lights."
HARRIS (infinite patience). Say it.

MARVIN. Lights.

HARRIS. Go ahead.

DODIE. So there I was in this elevator . . . only it was a sort of carousel, too . . . and on the horse next to mine . . . going up and down . . . I bet you can't guess who was there.

KIM (totally bored). You win!

DODIE. Well, it was a little vague but it was either Johnny Carson (or other popular entertainer), or the President.

SHEB. I don't know how anyone could tell 'em apart.

DODIE. And you know what he said? He said to me, "Dodie, you've got to put on some weight. You have very broad shoulders."

STU (coming downstage). This is a complete waste of time.

JERRY. If the subject is here and now problems, I don't see how Dodie's dreams fit in.

DODIE. Well, it was just last night and nobody else was saying anything.

KIM. It seems to me that if Mr. Paul Tobin is the great father figure, he could get his head together and direct the group into some subject that has some meaning.

PAUL. You sound angry.

KIM (correcting him). Bored.

PAUL. Why do you think I'm a father figure? (She doesn't answer.) Do you need your father to tell you what to do?

KIM. He can't run his own life. Who needs him to tell me how to run mine?

SHEB. Anybody bring a frisbee?

STU. You're costing the taxpayers a lot of money to sit here and say nothing.

KIM (to STU). But that's the bit. We're supposed to do the talking.

STU. But you just said . . . look, I'm agreeing with

　　　　you.

KIM. Then I must've been wrong.

STU. That's ridiculous.

KIM (thinking it out). No. Yes, it is. Ridiculous.
　　　　I was right in the first place. I'm into the
　　　　value of talking and you're talking about
　　　　money. That's all you ever think about.
　　　　Money.

STU. How do you know what I think about? You
　　　　don't even know me.

KIM. To know one parent is to know them all! (She
　　　　slams over to the chair beside CLAIRE and
　　　　sits.)

CLAIRE (to ADELE, wisely). That child is going
　　　　through a phase. (Annoyed, KIM rises,
　　　　moves to chair between JERRY and BARBARA,
　　　　and sits.)

JERRY. It's very obvious this group is a quivering
　　　　mass of insecurities. She can't even sit
　　　　next to somebody that's critical.

KIM. Go to hell! (She picks up this chair and moves
　　　　it to between SHEB and JANE.)

CLAIRE (a reproof). Language!

KIM (to JERRY, about CLAIRE). And take her with
　　　　you. (She sits.)

ACTRESS WHO PLAYS ADELE. You think it's all
　　　　right to say "hell"? (Everyone looks at
　　　　her, coming out of character. ACTOR WHO
　　　　PLAYS STU sits beside ACTRESS WHO
　　　　PLAYS CLAIRE.)

ACTOR WHO PLAYS SHEB. I say it every day.
　　　　Well, not on Sundays.

ACTRESS WHO PLAYS ADELE. I mean in a play.
　　　　In front of everyone.

ACTRESS WHO PLAYS CLAIRE. I think it's there
　　　　for Claire's reaction. To show she's a
　　　　hypocrite.

ACTOR WHO PLAYS TONY. There are more
　　　important things to change in this play.
HARRIS (to TONY, using his real name).
　　　————→ let us assume the playwright
　　　knows more than you do.
ACTOR WHO PLAYS TONY (uptight).　I don't know
　　　about that. I don't know how much he knows
　　　about the kind of problems, I . . . people
　　　like us have. He's messing with some
　　　pretty serious things.
HARRIS (surprised by his vehemence). Look, if
　　　this play really upsets you . . . if you'd
　　　like to change your mind and get out . . .
ACTOR WHO PLAYS TONY (sensitive). Why me?
　　　Why do you think that I, of all these people,
　　　can't do this play?
HARRIS. I don't. I just wanted to be sure you felt
　　　comfortable.
ACTOR WHO PLAYS TONY. I'm fine. I just think
　　　some of it is in bad taste.
ACTOR WHO PLAYS JERRY (after a pause). It's
　　　my line. (Resuming his characterization.)
　　　And besides, Kim's wrong.
STU. Are you agreeing with me?
JERRY (surprised himself). Crazy, isn't it? But how
　　　can anything definitive come out of an
　　　artificial situation where twelve people . . .
SHEB. What were you expecting? A miracle cure?
　　　(Going into a crusty old doctor characteriza-
　　　tion.) I say, Dr. Kildare, I believe you
　　　have isolated the manic depressive virus.
　　　What a giant step forward for the cuckoos
　　　of the world.
JERRY (losing his temper). Oh, shut up!
SHEB (in a fake German accent). *Ach du lieber* . .
　　　kindly Dr. Freud, dere, is losing his cool.

VICKIE.   You are not funny!

SHEB.   I'm doing my best.   Maybe this ain't my
         crowd.   (He sits.)

JERRY (going to PAUL).   He's destructive.   He keeps
         doing those corny bits.

PAUL.   Why are you telling me?   Would you like to
         tell him?

JERRY (to SHEB).   You're just trying to get atten-
         tion.

DON.   And why were you giving your lecture on
         comparative psychology or whatever that
         was?

JERRY (starting toward DON).   Completely different.

DODIE.   How?

JERRY (turning back).   I'm trying to help.   Why does
         it frighten all of you?   What are you afraid
         will be revealed about yourselves?

ADELE.   You're so busy helping us, you don't
         reveal very much about you.

KIM.   Oh, but he does.   He reveals he has a need
         for attention as much as-- (Referring to
         SHEB.)-- that dribble mouth.

STU.   This is really just a lot of talk.

DODIE.   It's more interesting than when no one was
         saying anything.

BARBARA.   You only get something out of a thing
         like this if you contribute to it.   If you don't
         enter into it, you can't blame us if you get
         nothing out of it.

JERRY (moving to her).   Who do you mean by us?

BARBARA.   I don't know . . . I suppose I meant
         teachers.

JERRY.   But we're supposed to be here just as
         people . . . not as representatives of our
         position in life.

BARBARA.   I know that.

JERRY.   So why do you insist on maintaining your

authority?

BARBARA. It's just . . . a habit.

JERRY. A habit or a real drive for power? A
    desire to keep the inferiors in their
    place?

SHEB. And he's off and running, folks. . . .

ADELE. Why are you hounding Barbara?

JERRY. I'm not. I'm trying to make her see what
    she's doing. Why does it bother you?

VICKIE. I think you're pushing Barbara the way
    you're suggesting teachers push us.

CLAIRE. And you're being very rude, besides.

KIM (rising). Rude? What is "rude"? (Impatiently,
    she walks upstage. JERRY sits in his
    former chair.)

CLAIRE. It's obvious you don't know. Most of
    you young people have lost respect
    for parents and teachers.

BARBARA. Respect has to be earned, Claire.

CLAIRE. Not earned. Learned. I would not
    accept that kind of behavior . . . that
    rude, pushy t⸺ from my son.

KIM (moving down in front of her). Your son?
    Is he Frank Newell?

CLAIRE (defensive). I'm not here to discuss my
    son.

KIM (laughing). I know what kind of behavior
    you accept from him.

CLAIRE (very angry). Will you be quiet? (A
    pause. Surprise at her reaction. KIM
    sits same chair.)

PAUL. Do you want to talk about your son,
    Claire?

CLAIRE. We're supposed to discuss here and
    now subjects, aren't we?

PAUL. Do you want to talk about your feeling toward

Kim or Jerry?

CLAIRE.　No.　We wouldn't get home before dawn.

STU.　I think we should break this up.

BARBARA.　It's not ten o'clock yet.

STU.　I mean break it up for good.

JANE (involuntarily, loud).　No! (They all turn, surprised, to look at her.) Oh, excuse me. But, no! (Coming out of character, the actress comes down to HARRIS, asking:) Why is this girl always saying "Excuse me"?

HARRIS.　She's insecure.

ACTRESS WHO PLAYS JANE.　About what?

HARRIS.　It is your job as an actress to find out about what.

ACTRESS WHO PLAYS DODIE (helpfully).　She's shy.

ACTRESS WHO PLAYS JANE.　Then she wouldn't have joined a here and now group.

ACTOR WHO PLAYS JERRY.　She's not that shy.

HARRIS.　May we continue?

ACTRESS WHO PLAYS JANE (as JANE, saying it as though she hates it as she walks back to her seat).　Oh, excuse me, but no. I don't want this to break up.

PAUL.　Why?

JANE.　It's too soon. Nobody's listening to anyone yet. You can't learn if you don't listen and everyone's just . . . just talking.

CLAIRE.　I've listened.

JANE.　Excuse me. . . . (As actress, commenting on line.) Yich. (As JANE.) Excuse me, but no!

KIM.　Right there, I think that girl has made a giant step forward.

JANE.　I came here because I thought people might listen. Not that I had anything that important to say . . . but I thought maybe they'd look at me. Hardly any of you are looking at me.

(It's true. They all turn to her.) I could
just as well have stayed home.

PAUL.   What did you want to get out of this, Jane?

JANE.   I don't know. Or I do, but it's hard to say.
I wanted to get a better idea of who I am by
being able to see what I looked like to other
people. Does that make sense?

ADELE.   Excellent sense.

CLAIRE.   I have a marvelous supportive idea. Why
don't we all give our instant, right off the
top of the head, opinion of Joan.

BARBARA. Jane!

CLAIRE (glaring at BARBARA). I'll start. She has
a pretty figure and lovely hair.

ADELE.   She seems to be a sweet girl. I don't feel
as though I know her.

SHEB.   This is a lousy idea, Claire. I pass.

STU.   Jane's a good kid. She's quiet.

KIM.   And that's a credit to a nation that has given
the world   the telephone, the soap opera
and Claire!

VICKIE.   I think Jane's very sensitive and essentially
a really good person.

JANE.   Thank you.

JERRY.   I think what we have here is a classic example of basic insecurities resulting in . . .

CLAIRE.   Please, young man, don't make another
speech. Just tell us what you think of . . .
(Can't remember the name.) . . . that girl.

JERRY.   She's shy.

ACTRESS WHO PLAYS DODIE (to JANE). See?

BARBARA.   That's true, but I think she realizes it
and is making a sincere effort to break out.

DODIE.   She's a very sweet, understanding person
with whom I could be friends.

CLAIRE (to TONY). You . . . you on the end.

TONY.   I . . . uh . . . I agree with them.

CLAIRE (disappointed). Oh.

JANE (sort of laughing). Well, I got a lot out of that.

PAUL. Did you get anything?

JANE. Proof. Proof of what I knew. People don't react to me because I'm not very interesting. I'm just sort of a vacuum walking around in a sweater and skirt.

VICKIE. That's not fair, Jane. We don't know you very well. Surely your friends see more in you . . .

JANE. I don't have friends. Why do you think I sat next to you last week?

VICKIE. Maybe you like me . . . maybe there was an empty chair . . .

JANE. Because I'd spoken to you at orchestra try-out. That's as close as I come to having friends.

CLAIRE. But your family, June . . .

JANE. Jane!

CLAIRE. Whatever . . . a girl can always rely on her mother.

JANE (smiling). Even my metronome goes out of rhythm. There is no one for me to fall back on.

PAUL. That's what I want you to do, Jane. Fall back on someone. (He takes her hand, moves her downstage.)

JANE. What do you mean?

PAUL. Literally . . . physically. (To others.) Will a few of you make a wall behind her? (She turns to look as VICKIE and BARBARA, then ADELE and DON, form a line shoulder to shoulder a little behind her. PAUL pulls her around so she can't see. As this happens:)

HARRIS. Everybody in the catching bit, drop your books. Fake your lines if you don't know them. (Those involved drop books.)

PAUL (to JANE). Don't look! Close your eyes.
          Have the courage to rely on somebody
          being there . . . anybody being there . . .
          and let yourself fall backward.
JANE. I can't do that. I could injure my hand. My
          violin . . .
PAUL. Someone will catch you. Just believe they will.
JANE. No . . . no, I don't want to. . . .
VICKIE. Don't be scared, Jane. I'll catch you. I
          understand about your hands. I play, too.
JANE. Let somebody else do this.
PAUL. Why, Jane? How do you feel? Talk about
          what you're feeling.
JANE. Frightened. Alone and frightened.
STU (joining the line behind her). I'll catch you.
          I been catching kids for years.
JANE (now really upset). No. Father s don't . . .
          they never . . . you fall and you lie there
          and you hurt.
DON. That's not true. You . . . you have to count
          on your father. He's part of your team,
          isn't he?
CLAIRE (moving to JANE). Stop badgering this poor
          child. Now, Jean, dear, you don't have to
          do anything . . .
KIM (coming down beside CLAIRE). Stop proving
          what a good mother you are. . . .
JANE. I have a good mother . . . she just feels
          she ought to be with him on the business
          trips, don't you understand?
BARBARA (to CLAIRE). The important thing is to let
          her do it on her own.
JANE. I don't mind being left alone. I like it. They
          always leave very reliable people with me.
VICKIE. Try, Jane. There are people you can rely
          on even if you can't see them.
PAUL. What people are you talking about, Vickie?

VICKIE. Me!

PAUL. Tell her!

VICKIE. I want you to rely on me!

JANE. I can't . . .

SHEB (moving front of the line, facing out). Like this, baby. . . . Is anyone back there? (He falls backward like an ironing board, yelling:) Geronimo! (STU makes a reflex grab, just catching him.)

STU. You could've killed yourself.

CLAIRE (angry). That's not what that child wants to hear! (Pushing SHEB into the line.) Just stand there! (She turns front. To JANE:) And I'm older than you! (She falls back. STU catches her. Defiantly:) It's fun! (She rises and grabs her back to ease a sudden pain.)

KIM (coming down in front of line). Neat-o, Claire! (She falls back. BARBARA catches her.)

JERRY (moving down). Somebody catch me.

DODIE (also coming down). And me. But I need two catchers! (They both fall. SHEB catches JERRY; DON and VICKIE catch DODIE.)

KIM. Come on in, the water's fine!

JANE (scared but game). All right . . . all right . . . here I go . . . (She falls. SHEB catches her.)

SHEB. Is it true Isaac Newton started like this?

JANE (looking at him). You? You're the most unreliable . . .

SHEB (pushing her up). Do it again!

VICKIE. Let me . . . (JANE falls, is caught by SHEB, VICKIE is caught by JERRY.)

PAUL. All right. That's enough. Let's talk about it. . . .

HARRIS (as they continue falling). But you don't stop . . . you keep going until the lights dim.

MARVIN. Lights. (Lights start to dim down. They
        continue falling.)
HARRIS. Keep it up - keep going.
ACTRESS WHO PLAYS CLAIRE (stops, making a
        joke, holding her back). Keep going? I
        may be in traction for weeks. . . .
        (Laughter.)

BLACKOUT

Scene 3

(The director's table and chair have been removed.
       The actors are in position for Scene Three.
       [See illustration.] No one carries playbooks
       any more except the stage managers.
       DODIE has a box of caramel corn into
       which she occasionally dips as the scene
       progresses. HARRIS stands C facing
       the actors, ELAINE and MARVIN at either
       side of him.)

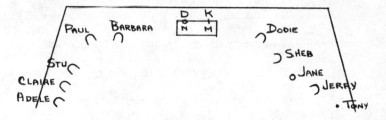

HARRIS. All right. Strict run-through, Scene
       Three. Keep going even if you make a
       mistake. I'm timing it. I'll take notes
       from front. Elaine and Marvin will prompt
       you, but I hope you don't need it. (ELAINE
       and MARVIN exit to opposite sides of the
       stage. HARRIS, if possible, goes down to
       theatre aisle and runs up and out, calling:)
       Lights! (The group is evidently in the
       middle of a session.)
ADELE. . . . and this morning at breakfast, she
       said she wanted us to serve liquor at her
       party.

Well, my husband said "no" immediately
. . . and it is a sweet sixteen party and
I don't blame him. Then Susan cried and
appealed to me and said all the others had
liquor . . . or at least beer . . . and I
don't know what to say . . .

JERRY. You never seem to know what to say.

ADELE. No?

JERRY. Absolutely not. You flip flop around every
issue that's raised. I don't know what you're
for.

ADELE (quietly). I don't know, either. Maybe that's
why I joined the group.

JERRY. It's nothing personal. I mean, you're as nice
as anybody else. I just think you're useless.

ADELE. Thanks.

JANE. But she's trying to find out who she is--what
she stands for.

JERRY. Cool. When she finds out, let her call me.

BARBARA. I thought the point of this was finding
out who we are.

JERRY. I know.

KIM (sarcastic). Y'know, that's kind of adorable.
How many people that you know even think
they know who they are?

DON. That kind of sarcastic attitude doesn't help
anybody.

SHEB. I think Jerry's a bluff. If he knew who he
was, he wouldn't be here. And if he does
know, what's he doing here? I think
Jerry's useless.

PAUL. Has it occurred to anybody that this group
seems very hostile?

DODIE. Oh, I don't think so. We're all just . . .
interested.

SHEB. Oh, yeah, fun! It's like jumping into a
river and playing water polo with the

        piranhas.

PAUL. Do you think we should talk about our need
        for attacking each other?

KIM. Personally, I'm polite all day in school. I
        only come around here for the relief of
        telling the truth.

DON. You're not telling the truth. You're just
        working off a lot of aggressions. Too bad
        there isn't a football team for girls. You
        can let off a lot of steam in a scrimmage.

KIM (angry). And you're smug! (He doesn't react.)
        Smug! You sit there acting like you're
        better than the rest of us . . . above all
        this! Well, you're a dumb, stupid jock.
        Maybe you can relate to a football but you
        can't relate to people.

DON (cool). Maybe there's nobody around worth
        relating to.

KIM. You're an ox! An ox with no feelings! I
        hate you. I hated you the minute you
        walked in here!

DODIE. I don't think that's true. Y'know what? I
        think she likes him.

SHEB. Why would she like him?

DODIE. Look at him. He's gorgeous.

KIM (agreeing). Gorgeous. So put him in a frame
        and hang him on a wall. I just put him
        down real hard. He doesn't even react.

DON. What do you expect me to do? Cry?

CLAIRE. Do you never cry? My son never cries.
        I'm not sure it's healthy.

KIM. Oh, no, Claire. Men don't cry. Emotions
        are feminine. (Whirling on DON.) Right?

DON. Right.

KIM. I broke my hand but I'll play the last ten
        minutes, coach. Then everybody'll dig
        my cool . . . see they got a real

American hero.

DON (beginning to anger). The team needed me, I
    played. That's the way I was brought up.
    My dad was in the Olympics . . .

KIM. Let me ask you something. Do you ever go
    out with girls?

DON. Sure I do! What are you getting at?

DODIE (poking SHEB). Ah hah! See!

KIM. So you date. But if you have no emotions, how
    do you feel about the chicks?

DON. Girls are . . . they're girls.

VICKIE. I hate that attitude!

DON. I like girls. But, I'm in high school. I'm not
    ready to get married.

JANE. But if you do go out with a girl, you should
    have some . . . some feeling for her.

DON. Look, I want to go to college and I want an
    athletic scholarship. I don't have time for
    . . . I'm in training. I can get a scholar-
    ship because I'm good. My dad worked with
    me since I'm a little kid. I've got ambitions
    that . . .

KIM (needling, mock innocent). Did your father ever
    tell you about the birds and the bees?

DON (really angry). Shut up about my father! He's got
    two silver medals . . . Olympic medals. He's
    OK and so am I.

JERRY. Can't you admit that all your cool . . . your
    aloofness . . . that's all a defense?

KIM. Scared, baby? Scared you'll get a bigger hurt
    than a broken hand?

DON. I can take getting hurt. (Controlling himself,
    tightly, to all, not believing what he says
    but saying it to get the pressure off.) Maybe
    I should relate to people better. Thank you.
    All. Maybe I did learn something about my-
    self. (He rises and walks back, standing

faced away from the group.)

DODIE (going to him with caramel corn).   Would you like some caramel corn?

SHEB.   Dodie, what are you supposed to be? The stewardess? (In a fun voice.) Coffee, tea or caramel corn?

DODIE.   I just thought . . .

JERRY.   Well, cut it out. We don't want your sympathy. We don't want your constant picnic. We want your feelings, if you have any.

DODIE.   I don't. (She starts back to her chair.)

VICKIE.   Then what are you doing here?

DODIE.   I don't have anywhere else to go. (She sits again.)

ADELE.   That can't be true.

DODIE (half laughing).   This is . . . a way of getting out of the house. It's . . . it's pretending I've got somewhere I have to be.

CLAIRE.   I can't believe a sweet, attractive girl like you doesn't have . . .

DODIE.   Oh, stop that! You sound like my mother. (DON turns, beginning to listen.)

CLAIRE.   Well, darling, your mother has had more experience . . .

DODIE (sharply).   My mother walks through life blindfolded. If she could see me, would she tell me I'm beautiful and feed me spaghetti at the same time?

CLAIRE.   You have many attractive . . .

BARBARA.   You don't have to eat the spaghetti.

DODIE.   I know I don't. Do you think I'm stupid as well as ugly?

VICKIE.   You're not ugly. Nobody has to be ugly. Explain to your mother. Make her see. Then, if you just fix up a little . . . take off some . . .

DODIE (for the first time forceful, really angry).

Don't you pity me! You will never understand
what it's like to be a fat freak!

ADELE. Dodie!

DODIE (more calmly). My mom and I, we're more
like girl friends than mother and daughter.
She always says it. There's nobody except
the two of us . . . and that's all we need.
Just the two of us. She's had a very rough
. . . I'm not fighting with my mother.

VICKIE. I didn't mean . . . I meant to say everyone
has to have a life of their own. You have to
let your mother know you deserve that.

DODIE (quietly). I know that I will never be able to
get married . . . (Defensively.) Well, I
don't really care that much because . . .
because I've never had a date. Never. So
if you can't get even a date, you certainly
aren't going to get a husband, right? But
even if I did . . . I mean, what would happen
to Mom? You see, he married . . . my
father married again . . . in California or
Oregon or somewhere and she's . . . well,
if I ever got married or anything, she'd be
all alone and I can't . . . so, y'see, I might
just as well eat the spaghetti and enjoy it,
right? 'Cause I'm not really losing anything
by it. (Looking into her hands.) Y'know what?
Nobody ever kissed me. Ever. (The others
look at her. DON moves to her side, sinks
to his knees, embraces her and kisses her.
They hold it a moment, then she breaks it,
putting her head on his shoulder, crying.
PAUL rises.)

PAUL. It's 10:30. (He moves to DON, pats his shoulder in thanks. STU and JANE rise, prepar-
ing to leave. TONY and KIM walk almost off

L, pausing to listen when DON begins.)

DON. I don't get involved. I don't even try, either, Dodie, 'cause I figure if somebody knew me, if I let someone know me real well, they'd see how . . . well, how I can't really do things right. But . . . maybe it's easier, Dodie, to . . . to say to somebody, I'm dumb . . . or I fumbled. Or I ran when I should've passed. Maybe that's easier than the other way. My God, my hand hurt. I wanted to get out of that game . . . but he was up there in the stands and you know what he said after? He said, "It was your left hand. If you threw a pass with your right, there was a man in the clear and you'd've won the game." My God, it hurt! (There is a pause. Then DODIE rises and runs off L.)

STU. I've got an early appointment . . . (He starts L. KIM and TONY go off. STU exits behind them. DON rises and sits in Dodie's chair, quietly.)

ADELE (to CLAIRE, as they rise and start L). I guess I'm not very forceful. It's the first problem I've brought up and everyone else just took over.

PAUL. I'm sorry, Adele. The meeting sort of got away from us. Bring it up again next week.

ADELE. The party's Saturday. I'll think of something. (She starts off.)

CLAIRE (following her). I'll tell you exactly what to do. . . . (They are gone.)

JERRY. I thought she would. (He goes off.)

JANE. Good night. (She exits.)

PAUL. You need a lift, Don? (DON shakes his head "No".)

VICKIE. It was a good session, Paul. (She goes off with SHEB.)

PAUL (to them). G'night. . . . Thanks, Don. (He
        goes off with BARBARA.)

(As soon as DON is alone, he begins to cry softly.
        After a second, KIM returns, goes to him
        and puts her arm around his shoulders. He
        turns and embraces her for a second. Then
        he rises and, arms around each other, they
        go off.)

                    BLACKOUT

Scene 4

(In the darkness, from the back of the theatre--or
over a loudspeaker--we hear:)

HARRIS. This is a dress rehearsal, Elaine. What's
the delay? Start Scene Four!

(ELAINE appears stage R carrying a flashlight,
flashing it out front.)

ELAINE. Are you out there, Mr. Harris?
HARRIS. Where else would I be? Why have you
stopped?
ELAINE (flashing light on her own face). I'm sorry.
After Scene Three we blew a fuse.
HARRIS. Then change it!
ELAINE. I did. (She licks a burnt finger.) You sup-
pose there's any butter in the cafeteria?
HARRIS. Please go on.
ELAINE (snappish, calling). Scene Four! (She exits.
Lights come up.)

(In this scene actors are now wearing "play" costumes.
Only SHEB is on stage. He is seated and
seems to be waiting with a certain amount of
tension. He hears a noise off L and stands,
trying to see who is coming. DODIE enters.)

SHEB (disappointed). Oh.
DODIE (hearing the disappointment, sarcastic). Nice
to see you, too. (She sits, takes a lollypop
from her purse and begins to eat it.)

(SHEB paces, looking up when he hears someone else,

47

who proves to be JANE, entering L. He looks
away, disinterested. JANE sits beside
DODIE.)

JANE. I'm early 'cause I was afraid I'd be late.
DODIE. Huh?
JANE. I mean, I never got home after school. I'm
    on the program committee for the orchestra's
    Christmas concert and we had such an argu-
    ment about Bela Bartok, by the time we fin-
    ished, I figured if I went home I'd be late
    getting back but if I just stayed I'd be early.
    So I haven't eaten. I didn't practice today
    and I never liked Bela Bartok anyway. (She
    smiles.) It's fun.

(VICKIE enters L.)

VICKIE. Hi, girls. (She heads toward them, but
    SHEB zooms over to her side, takes her arm
    and smoothly walks her across the stage away
    from them before she can sit.)
SHEB. Say, I didn't know you worked at Simon's.

(TONY enters. Takes his usual seat in the corner L.)

VICKIE. Just Saturdays. I help out in the Books and
    Records Department.
SHEB. That's cool. I was there buying a Barbie wed-
    ding dress. It's my kid sister's birthday.
    For what they cost I could practically have
    bought a wedding dress for her. (VICKIE
    smiles.) Only where would she wear it?
    It's a little heavy for Brownie meetings.
VICKIE. Why didn't you say hello?
SHEB. You had a customer.

(CLAIRE and ADELE enter together.)

CLAIRE (to ADELE, continuing a conversation).   So I said to her, "You've been here a whole week and you've never scrubbed the kitchen floor," and she said, "Mrs. Newell, I get down on my knees for no one but God."

ADELE.   So you fired her?

CLAIRE.   I couldn't. She quit.

SHEB (to VICKIE).   You talked to him a long time. He was a blond guy with a mustache. Tall. Who was he?

VICKIE.   I don't remember. A customer.

SHEB.   I've got the lead in the Senior class play. It's a comedy.

(JERRY enters, starts toward SHEB and VICKIE.)

VICKIE.   Great!

JERRY (reaching them).   Hi, Vickie.

SHEB (moving her DR, to JERRY).   Private conversation. (JERRY, a little miffed, sits.) We start rehearsing next week. Saturday night there's a party. You know . . . meet each other . . . talk about what we're going to do . . . and . . . y'know . . . kid around. Go with me?

VICKIE.   I don't get out of work till seven.

SHEB.   Crazy!

(SHEB and VICKIE continue to talk as BARBARA enters. Seeing TONY, she moves directly to him.)

BARBARA.   Tony . . .

TONY.   Yes, Miss Ekstrom?

BARBARA. I saw you . . . sitting in the auditorium
          this week.
TONY. Yes?
BARBARA. Every day.
TONY. I . . . I got a lot of studying to catch up on.

(STU enters, takes a seat.)

BARBARA. I looked up your program, Tony. I
          checked with some of your teachers.
TONY. It's not your business . . .
BARBARA. I wasn't spying, Tony. I just wondered.
          . . . You haven't been to any of your classes
          in weeks.
TONY. I got a lot of catching up to do.
BARBARA. You can't catch up cutting classes. If
          . . . Tony, if you need any help, I . . .
TONY (turning her off). Thanks a lot, Miss Ekstrom.
          Yeah . . . I'll . . . I guess I'm caught up.
          I'll be going back.
BARBARA. If there's something I can do . . .
TONY. I'll let you know. Thanks.

(PAUL enters.)

PAUL. Hi. Everybody here?
DODIE. Kim isn't.
JANE. And Don.
PAUL. Well, they'll turn up. Let's get started.
          Everybody want to sit down? (Those who are
          not sitting down, do.)

(DON and KIM enter L. He has his hand in a bandage
          and a sling. SHEB escorts VICKIE to bench
          from R; DON takes KIM to bench from L.
          The four arrive together.)

DON (politely). Sorry. (SHEB bows, VICKIE sits
       right on bench, KIM left on bench, boys
       on chairs beside them.)

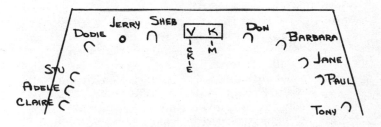

PAUL. I'd like to start with a question tonight. I
       want each of you to answer it with the
       first thing that comes into your mind. Don't
       analyze. Just speak. What is the most
       difficult problem you face in your life?
CLAIRE. Getting a good cleaning lady! (They all
       look at her as though she was crazy.)
SHEB. Who was that general said "war is hell"?
CLAIRE (embarrassed). Well . . . it is . . . well,
       it's difficult.
DODIE. I guess everybody knows my worst problem.
       (Holds up lollypop.) OK. I'm giving it up
       for good! (She throws it into the wings.)
BARBARA. That's an easy question for me. It's
       the whole point of my being in this group.
       My worst problem is . . . being unable to
       get through to people.
DON. To who?
BARBARA (correcting automatically). To whom?
       Students, mostly. I don't mean I can't get
       through to most students . . . but now and
       then, there's one I just can't reach. I

　　　　don't know if it's my fault or theirs. Or
　　　　whether it's nobody's fault at all.
VICKIE.　Maybe they just don't want to be reached?
STU.　Maybe if you got through, you'd discover there
　　　　was nobody there.
BARBARA.　I know that. But what distresses me . . .
　　　　is maybe I'm missing the one . . . the one
　　　　who really has something, if somebody
　　　　could get to it.
ADELE.　But with so many pupils, no one could
　　　　fault you if, with a difficult one . . .
BARBARA.　I've told myself that. But then, I think
　　　　. . . maybe Dr. Schweitzer was difficult
　　　　in high school. What if his teacher . . .
　　　　or Einstein's . . . or anybody's . . . didn't
　　　　bother to try? Wouldn't that be a terrible
　　　　waste? I'm so afraid of waste, Paul.
PAUL.　You're trying to say something else.
BARBARA.　Yes. Why haven't you made him speak?
　　　　(She points to TONY.)
PAUL.　I don't make anyone do anything. If you're
　　　　worried about Tony, do something about it.
BARBARA (to TONY).　Don't you have something to
　　　　say?
TONY.　No. Nothing.
BARBARA.　You haven't said a word . . . and this is
　　　　the fourth meeting.
DODIE.　You never even take any candy.
TONY.　I'm listening. It's OK.
BARBARA.　But how do you feel? What are you feeling?
　　　　What's the most difficult problem in your
　　　　life, Tony? (TONY shrugs.) Please . . .
TONY (mumbling).　Everything.
CLAIRE.　What? What did he say?
PAUL.　Did you say "everything"?
TONY.　Look . . . Look . . . I have no opinion.
JERRY.　But you've listened. What did you think

            about what Barbara said?
VICKIE.   You're one of the group.
TONY.   No. No, I'm not.
KIM.   You've been at every session. You know a lot
            about us. We don't have a clue about you.
TONY.   You know each other. You're friends.
PAUL.   That's not true. No one knew anyone else
            before we started.
TONY.   I am not _in_. And I don't want to be _in._
DON.   Nobody forced you to come.
JANE.   I understand what he means. No one will
            laugh at you or anything, Tony.
ADELE.   Why don't you try to join us?
TONY.   I'm going to leave school anyway.
BARBARA.   No! You mustn't!
TONY.   It doesn't mean anything. Like, it's good
            for some guys, but . . . other people . . .
            they don't get in on things.
PAUL.   Everybody, would you get up and form a
            circle . . . not Tony . . . everyone else.
            (They rise, forming a loose circle at C.)
            Would you say, Tony, that they are a
            circle in which you don't belong?
TONY (nodding).   Yes. Some people are loners.
            I like my own time. Like my brother,
            he belonged. Straight A's. Not me. I
            don't belong in their circle. I don't belong
            in school.
PAUL.   What do you want to do, Tony?
TONY.   Get a job. Get some money.
PAUL.   You think people will accept you more?
TONY.   I don't care if they accept me. Who are they?
            I want to do my own thing . . . when I want to.
PAUL (to the others, now in circle).   Make that a
            tight circle. Cross arms over the next
            person's neck. I want that circle very

       tight. (They do as he asks.) Now, Tony,
       try to break into that circle.

TONY. Forget it.

PAUL. Why not?

TONY. I could hurt somebody. There's women
       there.

PAUL. That's an excuse.

TONY. Nah. I won't do it. I can't.

PAUL. Tony, I want you to switch roles with me.
       I want you to be Paul and I'll be Tony. Do
       you understand, I'm speaking as Tony now
       and you are me, Paul. I am Tony and I can't
       get into the circle, Paul.

TONY (as PAUL). Then get out of here. What are
       you doing here, anyway?

PAUL (as Tony). I came because I am afraid.

TONY (as Paul). You're chicken, Tony.

PAUL (as Tony). Why am I like this, Paul? Why won't
       I even try?

TONY (as Paul). 'Cause of Lou. You know they all
       compare you to Lou. All the teachers here
       know you're not as good as your brother.
       He won the awards . . . valedictorian . . .
       everything. You're not in that class.

PAUL (as Tony). But I'd like to be. If I could try to
       be as good as Lou . . .

TONY (as Paul). You're crazy. With what? Lou's
       got the brains. When Poppa was dying, it
       was Lou he talked to. Lou he told to take
       care of Momma and take care of me.

PAUL. Not you. I'm Tony. He told Lou to take care
       of me.

TONY. 'Cause you can't even take care of yourself.
       Poppa knew it. From the grave he reminds
       me every day. Lou . . . Lou got the top
       marks. Lou has the good job. Lou brings
       the money to Momma. Momma loves him.

PAUL. And Momma doesn't love me. Nobody does.

TONY. Why should they? You're a miserable nothing. Break into that circle? You can't even say "hello" to these people!

PAUL. Nobody wants to say "hello" to me. Why should I have to break into a circle? If they wanted me there, they'd open up for me.

TONY. D'ya ever ask 'em to? You don't even have the guts to ask 'em to open up. Maybe they don't even know you want in. How can you expect help when you're too stupid to ask for it?

PAUL. Why should I let them turn me down? They don't want to help me any more than you do!

TONY. I want to help you!

PAUL. Then tell me what to do.

TONY. Break into the circle. Dammit, try to break into the circle.

PAUL. All right. Switch back. I'm Paul. You're Tony. Break into the circle. I want you to break into the circle!

TONY. OK, already! (Almost hysterical, he rushes to the downstage side of the circle where STU and JERRY are side by side, arms around each other's neck. TONY pulls on their arms, really struggling to break the grip.)

PAUL. Don't make it easy! Hang on, Jerry, make him work for it.

TONY. Dammit, open up. Open up! Let me in! (JANE, very moved, breaks the circle on the side at R.)

JANE. Here, Tony . . .

TONY. Not good enough! I want to break in here! (He pulls Jerry's arm down and pushes him aside, breaking into the circle. Almost hysterical, between laughing and crying, he stands in the center of the circle.)

I can. I can, Paul, I can!
PAUL (calm, smiling, pleased with Tony). OK.
     I'll see you all next Thursday. Eight o'clock.

BLACKOUT

Scene 5

(This next segment should be played as though backstage. Your theatre will determine where
best to play it. It can be at the extreme
side of the stage . . . possibly at the front
of one aisle. If there is light spill, use it;
if not, let HARRIS and MARVIN carry
flashlights and light each other's faces.
HARRIS also carries a clipboard to which
he refers. HARRIS appears first. It is
mid-performance. They talk quickly,
urgently.)

HARRIS. Marvin!
MARVIN (appearing). How's it going?
HARRIS. Very well.
MARVIN. Does the audience like it?
HARRIS. I think so. Will you tell Stu to talk a little
louder . . . remind Claire not to turn her
back to the audience, and tell Barbara to
put on a little more lipstick if she gets the
chance. . . . And tell Tony to keep his
energy up in the next scene. . . .
MARVIN. Right!
HARRIS. Get back . . . they should be starting
Scene Five. (They run off. Stage lights
come up.)

(It is the beginning of a session. Don's hand is now
in a bandage but he has discarded the sling.
Everyone is seated except PAUL, who
stands stage R holding a stop watch in
one hand, the other hand raised.)

PAUL. You have ten seconds. One . . . two . . .
         three . . . go!

(The object of what they are doing is to form a line.
         JERRY, KIM and SHEB immediately head
         toward Paul, for the head of the line.
         BARBARA and VICKIE move quickly, but
         not racing, in that direction. When they
         see a pushing contest start between JERRY
         and SHEB, they blend back a bit. ADELE
         moves at a lady-like pace somewhere toward
         the middle of the line. DON, going a bit
         more slowly, gets there before ADELE.
         TONY and JANE move toward the back of
         the line at L. DODIE comes downstage of
         forming line and indecisively moves up and
         down, not knowing where she fits in. CLAIRE
         and STU remain seated in last two chairs R.
         JERRY reaches the spot in front of PAUL first,
         almost immediately followed by SHEB and KIM.
         SHEB pushes JERRY out of first place physi-
         cally. KIM hangs back watching. All of
         this happens very quickly.)

JERRY. I was here first.
SHEB. He didn't say who was fast, he said who was
         dominant.
JERRY. Clowns are never dominant!
SHEB. Well, I'm here, now! (JERRY pushes him.
         SHEB shoves back. There's a little shoving
         battle. Meanwhile, BARBARA and VICKIE
         fall into line behind them, leaving a slight
         space to avoid the scuffle. DON and ADELE
         have moved to the space behind VICKIE at the
         same time, and DON politely steps back for
         ADELE. TONY moves behind DON, and JANE

behind TONY. DODIE still moves inde-
cisively between VICKIE and JANE.)

PAUL (putting his hand down). OK. Everybody
freeze! (There is a last-minute rush.
JERRY gives SHEB a firm push, SHEB falls
back and JERRY takes first place. KIM
rushes in behind him, holding on to his
shoulders so SHEB is forced to take third
place. Then come BARBARA, VICKIE,
ADELE, TONY (who has moved up), DON,
JANE and DODIE, who, giving up, has taken
last place. When they are settled:)
SHEB (loud whisper to JERRY). Cheater! (JERRY
smiles at him condescendingly.)
PAUL (walking downstage of line). Very interesting.
TONY (meaning CLAIRE and STU). They weren't
even in it.
CLAIRE. Children's games, darling.
BARBARA. Well, either you participate in this fully
or what are you doing here?
SHEB. If everyone isn't in it, it doesn't count! (A
bad loser, he leaves the line, moves R.)
JERRY. If you don't win, it doesn't count.
SHEB (turning back to fight). Listen, you big mouth.
(He throws a punch at JERRY; JERRY puts
up his fists. PAUL rushes back and grabs
JERRY as STU runs down to grab SHEB.)
PAUL. No fist fights.
STU (pulling SHEB further R, to BARBARA). That's
why I didn't play. I'm a grown man. I'm
not going to push kids around.
KIM. Why bother here? You can do that at home.
(STU glares at her.)
BARBARA (to SHEB). The idea was who was a
dominant personality. Not who could push
into line first.

STU. Exactly. And I don't think I need to prove
       that I am more dominant than a bunch of
       high school kids.

JERRY. But if you were, wouldn't you be in the
       front of the line? How you doing at the
       office, Stu? Take a lot of guff from your
       boss? (STU glares at him, moves away.)

ADELE. Well, I don't feel very dominant . . . or
       very passive, either . . . and I came out
       right in the middle of the line. That does
       seem to prove something.

SHEB. The whole thing's a bummer. Look at the
       big football hero. The iron man in the
       scrimmage, between the quietest guy in
       the group and a 98-pound girl violinist.

VICKIE (to DON). Yes. I always thought you were
       very . . . you know . . . aggressive.

KIM (snide). Only in a negative way.

DON. In sports you're supposed to be aggressive.
       Off the field . . . well, I don't like pushy
       people.

DODIE (to KIM). What do you mean, negative
       aggressive?

KIM. I mean he's going to play his game his way.
       If it's somebody else's football he'll sit
       on the sidelines. Firmly. Being aggressively
       negative. Or just plain chicken.

DON (angry). Maybe I don't like dominating females.
       Maybe I do get negative when I'm out with
       a girl and she acts like one of the boys.

KIM. What would you know about being out with
       girls?

DON. What do you mean by that?

KIM. I never heard any girl in this school say she
       dated you. Do you go out at all, or are you
       afraid to compete there, back of the line,
       submissive football hero?

SHEB. Oh, oh! I think we've stumbled on to some-
        thing personal.

PAUL. Do you want to talk about it?

DON. No. No, it's nothing.

KIM. Less than that. He's hopeless. I fccl sorry
        for him.

DON. Sorry for me? Dammit, she tried to get me
        to turn on.

STU. Drugs?

DON. Well, what do you think?

KIM. You don't have to worry about him. He's so
        uptight he wouldn't eat an ice cream cone
        without a lab report.

STU. Are you pushing?

KIM. I don't have to. It was purely social, Stu.
        I got enough to give the stuff away.

ADELE. Then why? Why try to get Don involved?

KIM. I thought it might turn him into a human.

DON. You want to blow your life, that's up to you.
        But leave me out of it.

KIM. I thought those muscles meant there was a
        man inside that shirt. You're not even a
        little boy. You're a wind-up doll. Your
        father turns the switch and you do a hundred
        push-ups.

CLAIRE (very upset, moving to KIM). You . . . you
        should be ashamed to show your face among
        decent people. You . . . you should be
        put away.

KIM. That's what you call transference, isn't it,
        Paul? Claire is saying to me what she
        can't say to her own son.

CLAIRE. My son! My son wouldn't go near a girl
        like you!

KIM. No? Where do you think I buy the stuff, Claire?

CLAIRE. That's a lie! Frank has never . . . he's
        a very good son. I've never had a moment's

trouble from him. He's always been . . .
I have been blessed with my son.

KIM.   You live with him! Can't you see what he's like?
You're lying to yourself! You're so busy
playing the Better Homes and Gardens
Mother of the Year, you don't even know where
your son is at.

CLAIRE.   It's not true! I don't want to hear. Stop
her!

STU (grabbing Kim's shoulders).   That's enough of
that!

CLAIRE.   She's like all of them . . . trying to shift
the blame for what she's doing on to somebody else.

STU (to PAUL).   Claire's right. What are you
going to do about this?

PAUL.   Do? What do you want me to do?

STU.   It's obvious. You go to your boss . . . you
go right up to the principal's office and you
tell George Lassiter what this kid--(Meaning
KIM.)--is doing.

CLAIRE.   You won't say anything about Frank? It
isn't true. Really.

BARBARA (to STU).   What happens inside this group
is supposed to be confidential. This group
won't work if we feel what is said in this
room is going to be repeated outside.

STU.   Who the hell cares if the group works? All
these cockeyed, new-fangled ideas. Human
relations groups. Guidance counselors.
Don't punish the kids, let them find themselves. OK. They've found themselves
. . . and what have they found? Drugs!
Liquor! Sex! (To KIM.) Oh, no, baby.
You're not going to run around loose if I've
got anything to say about it. Maybe you're
not pushing now, but maybe you start

next week. Maybe you're out after my kid
next.

KIM. If she wants it, she's entitled. And she
certainly knows where to get it.

STU. That tears it. (He starts L.)

TONY (moving into his path). Please don't go,
Mr. Ainsley . . .

STU. Oh, I'm going. I'm going 'cause I need a stiff
drink and then I'm going to see George
Lassiter and give him some idea of what's
going on in his school.

SHEB. Drink it, Daddy, but don't smoke it.

STU (starting back to him). Don't you get wise
with me, you young punk.

JANE (coming between them). Running out isn't
going to help.

STU. Maybe not you . . . maybe not him--(Pointing
to PAUL.)--but it's going to make me feel
better. (He starts out again. TONY
moves in, blocking him.)

TONY (very tense). Jane's right. You have to stay
and talk about it.

STU. What for? I've been coming here for five
weeks. That's time enough to write the
Declaration of Independence. And all I've
heard is a lot of drivel. Nobody's done
anything. Nothing's been accomplished.
(Starting around TONY.) Life is too short
. . . (TONY holds STU physically. In the
following speech, ACTOR WHO PLAYS
TONY becomes increasingly upset. While
he clings to the lines of his part he has
difficulty getting them out. Through the speech
a feeling of confusion--a loss of where he is--
builds.)

TONY. Don't go. Please. It's like . . . it helps . . .
this place . . . these people, they help. I

found a group I belong in. I . . . I . . .
(The other actors begin to get nervous,
sensing something is wrong with ACTOR
WHO PLAYS TONY. While they don't
leave their parts, they must convey a
feeling of the unexpected happening.) I
found a group I belong in. . . . I never
did . . . before . . . some place I'm home
. . . I have . . . I must . . . (A frantic
plea.) Listen!

STU. I've listened enough! Get out of my way!
(He shoves TONY.)

ACTOR WHO PLAYS TONY (now losing control,
going off into his own problem, forgetting
he is in a play at all).   You never listened.
Not now! Not ever! You're like my father.
(He grabs at STU almost as though he wants
to choke him. He continues talking, almost
babbling, as ACTOR WHO PLAYS PAUL
and ACTOR WHO PLAYS JERRY try to pull
him away from ACTOR WHO PLAYS STU.
The other actors look horrified.)   You act
just like he does. You never listen. You
never even look at your kids.

ACTOR WHO PLAYS PAUL.   Cut it out_____
(He uses ACTOR WHO PLAYS TONY'S
name.)

ACTOR WHO PLAYS TONY (going right on, not
waiting for other lines, blending his
speeches together).   You lie to yourselves.
You pretend it's the way you want it to be.
. . . (By now ACTOR WHO PLAYS JERRY
and ACTOR WHO PLAYS PAUL have
pulled him off STU and are holding him
back.) Somebody says something and you
go right on like they weren't even there!

ACTOR WHO PLAYS STU (trying to calm him).

I'm sorry . . .

ACTOR WHO PLAYS TONY (right on). You don't
        consider how they are . . . what we want
        . . .

ACTOR WHO PLAYS JERRY (trying to retain play).
        Tony . . . calm down . . . remember where
        you are.

ACTOR WHO PLAYS TONY. I don't care about this
        play. I hate it. It's too close to the truth
        but it isn't the truth. I'm what's true. Me!

ACTOR WHO PLAYS PAUL (calling off). Pull the
        curtain!

ACTRESS WHO PLAYS CLAIRE (moving to TONY at
        the same time, putting an arm around him
        and trying to calm him). Come on,_____
        (Uses his real name.) Let's get a drink of
        water. . . .

ACTOR WHO PLAYS TONY (continuing through above).
        I know him . . . Stu is my father . . . he
        doesn't know anything about me . . . (To
        CLAIRE.) Let me alone.

ACTOR WHO PLAYS PAUL (calling off). Marvin,
        will you pull the curtain!

ACTOR WHO PLAYS TONY (continuing). I don't
        want anything from him . . . I just want him
        to see me . . . see who I am. That's all
        I want. I just want him to see me! (He
        begins to cry; spent, he leans his face on
        CLAIRE's shoulder.)

ACTRESS WHO PLAYS BARBARA (shocked). He
        was right. We shouldn't have done this play.
        It is too upsetting.

(ELAINE enters R. ACTOR WHO PLAYS PAUL
        rushes to her.)

ACTOR WHO PLAYS PAUL. Close the curtain!

(ACTRESS WHO PLAYS CLAIRE walks
ACTOR WHO PLAYS TONY off L.)

ELAINE. What about the rest of the play?

ACTRESS WHO PLAYS BARBARA. Tell them it's
intermission. (CURTAIN begins to close
slowly.)

ELAINE. There is no intermission . . .

ACTRESS WHO PLAYS BARBARA. There is toinght.
And get Mr. Harris back here. (ELAINE
nods and, slightly dazed, comes downstage
as the curtain closes behind her.)

ELAINE (nervous, direct to audience). Uh . . .
would you . . . uh . . . take a break now?
I mean, we're going to have an intermission
. . . and we'll . . . uh . . . we'll go on
with the play in . . . uh . . . I guess in
fifteen minutes. You come back then. We've
had a little . . . technical trouble . . .
and . . . and, Mr. Harris, would you
come backstage, please? Somebody wants
to talk to you. (Calls off to wings.) House
lights, Marvin. (As they come up.) Uh . . .
fifteen minutes. Uh, thank you. (She goes
off.)

INTERMISSION

Scene 6

(The house lights dim down half way and ELAINE
        appears through the center of the curtain.
        She carries a piece of paper with a written
        announcement on it.)

ELAINE (to the audience, in desperate nerves and
        embarrassment). Uh . . . good evening.
        I mean . . . y'got back . . . uh . . . (Not
        knowing how to continue, she refers to the
        paper and reads:) Ladies and gentlemen,
        we, the cast of "Here and Now" (Looking up.)
        --and me, too, I'm the stage manager . . .
        (Back to the paper.) uh . . . "Here and Now"
        would like to express our apologies for the
        unfortunate incident at the end of the last
        scene. Feelings of exhaustion due to the
        strenuous rehearsals of the last few weeks
        as well as the emotional content of the play
        . . . (Looking up, she adds on her own.)
        . . . and exams . . . (Reading again.) . . .
        tended, understandably, to upset some of
        the actors. We hope you will bear with
        us and remain for the . . . uh . . . remainder
        of the performance. Thank you. (She starts
        to go off R.)
ACTOR WHO PLAYS JERRY (voice, from behind
        curtain). Tell 'em what happened!
ELAINE (to voice, stage whisper). They know what
        happened!
ACTOR WHO PLAYS JERRY (exasperated). What
        happened in the play!
ELAINE. Oh. (To audience.) Uh . . . well . . .
        y'see . . . like . . . uh . . . Stu . . .

y'know, the father? He walked out threatening
to tell the principal what happened. About
Kim . . . and then, Tony, he has a speech,
y'know, about how terrible he feels that the
group is breaking up . . . but then . . .
_____ (Actress Who Plays
Barbara's real name.) says . . . I mean
Barbara says, "We can't let it break up, " and
Tony says something like they're always
making you think they're going to help you
and then they don't and they can go . . . He
says something very rude . . . then Claire
starts yelling at him and Barbara yells at her
. . . it's really very dramatic, y'know? Exciting. It was great at dress rehearsal.
Then they notice Tony has run off and they all
start yelling and the curtain comes down . . .
and then . . . and then they do the next scene.
And that's this. (She points to the stage.)
Thank you. (She walks off R. House lights
go out completely.)

(Curtain rises. It is before the next meeting. ADELE
        and CLAIRE are alone on the stage. They
        are C, staring at each other. Evidently,
        CLAIRE has said something that upset and
        annoyed ADELE. ADELE looks at CLAIRE
        for a moment.)

ADELE (sighing). Oh, Claire . . . (Discouraged,
        she sits.)
CLAIRE (justifying herself). Well, I felt it was the
        only proper thing to do.
ADELE. But when Stu left last week, he said he
        was going to call Lassiter.
CLAIRE. And he did. He told me he expressed
        himself very firmly.

ADELE. Then why did you have to . . .

CLAIRE. Because I'm a mother and I think a mother's
voice adds . . . a dimension. Fathers just
fly off into a temper. But when a mother
says something it's a reasoned, logical
argument.

ADELE. And what did you say?

CLAIRE. I said that girl was a dreadful influence
and that she ought to be expelled and if he
was going to allow obviously disturbed
children into these human relations groups
then they were of no practical value.

ADELE (sarcastic). A very logical argument.

CLAIRE (somewhat calmed). That's what I thought.
(She sits.)

ADELE. But if you have come out against the
human relations groups, why did you come
tonight?

CLAIRE (again upset). Because! (She rises and
paces again.)

ADELE. "Because." (Annoyed and sarcastic.) I've
just got to say how much I admire your
reasoning, Claire.

CLAIRE (angry now). Because I had to see if that girl
had the gall to show her face again tonight.
And to find out if she was expelled.

ADELE. That girl needs reassurance. She has to
be taken in . . . not thrown out. Anyway,
she can't be expelled. There's no proof
she's done anything wrong.

CLAIRE (dismissing that as absurd). Proof! They
didn't need proof when . . . We don't
need proof. We know!

(DON enters L.)

CLAIRE. Have you seen Kim?

DON. I don't have any classes with her.

CLAIRE (irritable). After school? In the cafeteria?
         In the corridors? At MacDonald's?

DON (firmly). I don't see her. I'm working out with
         the team again. (He flexes his hand, now
         without bandage.)

ADELE. Oh, your hand is better.

(ADELE and DON begin to talk quietly to each other.
         CLAIRE sits alone. SHEB and VICKIE
         enter L.)

VICKIE. Do you think there'll be a session tonight?

SHEB. I don't much care.

VICKIE. No?

SHEB. No . . . I . . . I feel I got much more out of
         this group than I figured.

         (JERRY enters L, starts toward them.)

SHEB. Vickie . . . I . . . y'know what, Vickie?

JERRY (joining them). Say, I wasn't sure anybody'd
         be here tonight. . . .

SHEB (not wanting to be interrupted). D'you mind,
         Jerry? (He takes Vickie's arm and steers
         her further R, stopping and talking quietly
         to her.)

(DODIE enters L carrying a huge chocolate bar,
         half eaten.)

JERRY (after SHEB but really to himself). No, why
         should I mind? (To DODIE, as she passes
         him.) Say, I thought you were off candy.

DODIE (annoyed at being reminded). I am. But I'm
         terribly tense tonight! (She takes a big
         bite and joins DON and ADELE.)

JERRY (really to himself).   What's the matter with me?
I shower every day.

(BARBARA enters L.)

BARBARA (hearing him).   What?
JERRY (hostile).   Nothing.   Did you want to talk to
me?
BARBARA.   Not particularly.
JERRY.   Join the crowd.

(He moves upstage as PAUL enters L.)

PAUL.   Oh, I'm glad you're all here.   (They all look
around at him.)
VICKIE.   Not quite everybody.
PAUL.   Well, Tony won't be here.   Or Stu.
BARBARA.   What happened to Tony?
PAUL.   Dropped out.
ADELE.   Out of the group?
PAUL.   Out of school.
VICKIE.   Oh, I'm sorry.
SHEB.   Where'd he go?
PAUL.   I don't know.   His brother called me and said
he'd . . . well, disappeared.   He wanted to
know if I knew where he was or if anything
had happened here.
JERRY.   Should've told him to call Stu.
CLAIRE (imperiously).   So we are to understand that
Tony has run away?
ADELE (annoyed).   "Run away" makes him sound like
Tom Sawyer.   The boy is old enough to vote.
CLAIRE.   Nevertheless . . . he's gone . . . God
knows where, and you still intend to continue
this group? (There is a sudden, uncomfortable
pause.   Something has again gone wrong.
Nervously, ACTRESS WHO PLAYS CLAIRE

rephrases the cue line, louder.) Despite
everything, you intend to go on with the
group?
ACTOR WHO PLAYS JERRY (ad libbing, looking
        off into the wings). Wait a minute. We
        started without Jane. I think she's coming.
        There's Jane now. (There is another pause.)
ACTRESS WHO PLAYS VICKIE (giving up the pre-
        tense). Oh, brother! (She sits, disgusted.)

(ELAINE pokes her head out R, whispers.)

ELAINE. What is it?
ACTOR WHO PLAYS PAUL. _____
        (Actress Who Plays Jane's real name.) isn't
        here.
ELAINE (furious). Ohhh! (She disappears and we
        hear her calling the actress' name, off.
        The others stand around looking embarrassed.)

(ACTRESS WHO PLAYS JANE runs on, annoyed.)

ACTRESS WHO PLAYS JANE. Well, nobody told me
        you were starting!
ACTOR WHO PLAYS SHEB. Why weren't you listen-
        ing?
ACTRESS WHO PLAYS JANE (injured dignity). I was
        in the ladies' room. The real trouble with
        this play--there isn't time between scenes to
        comb your hair.
ACTRESS WHO PLAYS VICKIE (very annoyed). We're
        in the middle of a performance. You're
        being very unprofessional!
ACTRESS WHO PLAYS JANE (simple explanation).
        I'm an amateur.

(ELAINE pokes her head in again.)

ELAINE. All right? Can we finish the play?

ACTRESS WHO PLAYS JANE. What about _____
    (She uses Actor Who Plays Tony's real
    name.)

ELAINE. He's fine. He's ready to finish the play.

ACTRESS WHO PLAYS JANE. Well, so am I.
    Oh, if we'd done a nice musical, nobody
    would've flipped out.

ACTOR WHO PLAYS DON (rising). Let's go.

ACTOR WHO PLAYS JERRY. Please.

ACTRESS WHO PLAYS JANE (innocent). Well, I'm
    ready. Where are we?

ACTOR WHO PLAYS SHEB. Right up the creek.

ACTOR WHO PLAYS BARBARA. We were up to
    your line about going on with the group.

ELAINE. OK. Take it from Jane's line. (She
    disappears.)

ACTRESS WHO PLAYS JANE. I can't get back into
    the mood just like that.

ACTOR WHO PLAYS JERRY. Look at her! All of
    a sudden she's Sarah Bernhardt!

ACTRESS WHO PLAYS ADELE. Take it back to
    my line. "Run away" makes Tony sound
    like Tom Sawyer. The boy is old enough
    to vote.

CLAIRE. Nevertheless . . . he's gone . . . God
    knows where . . . and you still intend to
    continue this group?

JANE. We have to! Tony dropping out like that just
    proves how much we need it.

CLAIRE. No. It proves how inadequate this whole
    program is. That boy needed help. He
    must've realized it to sign up for this. But
    he needed real help . . . psychiatric help
    . . . and some amateur like you (Paul)
    . . . no matter how well-meaning . . . can
    with all the good will in the world seriously

damage someone, as perhaps Tony has been
damage.

BARBARA. Maybe Paul didn't succeed with Tony,
but he's trying. He's doing something.
Maybe he's helped Jane. Or me. Or even
you.

CLAIRE. I don't feel I need that much help.

PAUL. Then why did you join? And if you felt strongly
enough about it to call Lassiter after the
last time, why did you come back tonight?

CLAIRE. To find out what Lassiter did. Why wasn't
this meeting canceled? Why wasn't this
program dropped? Do we have to wait till
some child puts a gun to his head?

PAUL. This program probably will be canceled. The
school board doesn't meet for a few weeks
and . . . and Lassiter said I could finish
this session.

CLAIRE. Why?

PAUL. I don't know.

BARBARA. Because I went to him and I pleaded with
him. I explained what happened and why.

PAUL (touched). Did you do that?

BARBARA. I couldn't get him to say he'd support
continuing, but at least he said he'd let us
finish.

CLAIRE. Well, you are playing around with things
you have no right to play with, young woman.
It's time that the schools realized they are
here to teach the youngsters reading and
writing and chemistry and whatever. All
these new-fangled programs are nothing but
a deterrent to what they should be doing.

BARBARA. If we are going to ride to school on buses
rather than horse cars, we have to face the
fact that the world has changed . . . that
growing up today is difficult.

CLAIRE. It was always difficult. We managed.

SHEB. Yeah, but look at the condition you're in.

BARBARA. We cannot go back to the old ways.

ADELE. She's right. But I do wish they'd go back to the old math.

BARBARA. There are new problems. It's all much more complex. We aren't dealing with children, we are dealing with people. Young people--but people with drives and problems and confusions. And what do we do with them?

DON. You treat 'em like kids.

BARBARA. Right. We put them in schools where in the nature of the situation . . . with the teachers making rules . . . they have to feel incompetent . . . and then we expect them to behave in a mature way they haven't been permitted to develop.

ADELE. But, as parents, what are we supposed to do? If we don't make rules, if the teachers don't, where are they going to learn?

BARBARA. Rules won't help them clarify who and what they are. We have to help them learn what they want from life and what they need to put into it to get what they want. That counts at least as much as the multiplication tables!

CLAIRE. We must make rules. We have to watch them every minute . . . or they meet people who . . . other children who . . .

(KIM enters L, unobserved, and listens.)

CLAIRE. . . . who teach them the wrong things. That's where the schools have to help. Otherwise the good children go wrong if the bad ones aren't kept in control.

BARBARA. I'm a teacher. Not a warden.

CLAIRE. Then how can we as parents fight the bad
influences?

KIM. I think we first have to decide who the bad
influences are and what made them that
way.

CLAIRE. Perhaps you'd tell us how you became what
you are.

KIM. Right on. Then maybe you'll tell us how you
turned your son into the prime contact in
this school.

CLAIRE. That's a lie!

KIM. Oh, no. There isn't a kid in this school who
doesn't know it.

CLAIRE (to the adults, beginning to be very upset).
It's completely untrue. I admit there was
some gossip because of that incident when
they planted the stuff in his locker but he had
nothing to do with that. He wasn't expelled,
and that's proof. I made them see it was
planted. He has enemies. The other
children are jealous of Frank. I can understand that, because he's . . .

JERRY (loud, cutting through). It's true, Mrs. Newell.

CLAIRE (almost hysterical). Lies! Well, who'd believe
either of you, anyway? (To KIM.) I did
some checking on you. This fine example of
American youth . . . this accuser of my
Frank . . . she doesn't even live with her
parents . . . and you know why? Because
her own father threw her out!

KIM. And wasn't that a smart solution to his problem?
Now he can really pretend I don't exist.

CLAIRE. Well, there are some children that are
incorrigible.

KIM. And how did they get that way?

CLAIRE. Oh, they always blame the parents. That's

the easiest thing, isn't it?

ADELE (trying to be gentle).   If a child goes wrong,
a parent has to ask herself where she made
mistakes.

CLAIRE (justifying herself).   I gave him everything.
Everything he ever wanted.

ADELE.   It isn't easy.

CLAIRE.   I watched him.   Like a hawk.   I always knew
where he was.   I took him places myself.
I had no life of my own.   I was always making
plans for him.   For now.   For his future.
I neglected my husband and I devoted myself
to him . . . to protect him . . .

KIM.   So that's it.   He just wanted to get out from
under.

CLAIRE.   Oh, what do you know about it?

KIM.   I've got two of my own.   They did everything
for me.   Picked out my clothes, picked out
my friends.   I never saw a movie if they
didn't see it first.   Sure, they gave me an
allowance but if I bought a record or a
dress they didn't like, it mysteriously
disappeared.   If they thought I couldn't
even pick my own music, how did they
think I was going to manage my life?   If
they made me feel I had to do exactly what
they wanted before they'd give me love,
how did they think I'd behave with a boy?
If they made me feel like nothing, why are
they surprised that I am nothing?

CLAIRE (screaming).   My son is not like you!   I am
not like your parents.   I have a fine relationship with my son!   (She bursts into tears,
turning away from KIM.   KIM moves to
her, puts her hands on CLAIRE'S shoulders,
comfortingly.)

KIM.   If I could only have said that to my own mother.

CLAIRE. Don't touch me. You're a filthy little
        tramp! (KIM turns her around and slaps
        her. CLAIRE, shocked, stops crying,
        stares at her.)
KIM (evenly). You have to look at yourself, Mrs.
        Newell. You have to look at your son. You've
        got to see things the way they are. I've got
        to have a long look at myself, too.

BLACKOUT

(It is the beginning of the next session. PAUL stands
LC talking to the group. The others are
seated. See illustration:)

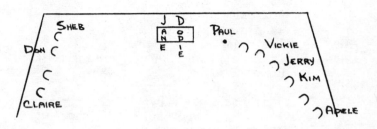

PAUL. I know you've all heard rumors of cancellation.
Well, no one knows anything yet. The school
board meets next Thursday, but I understand Mr. Ainsley has been talking to the
members one by one. Tony's disappearance
is against us. . . .

ADELE. Has anything been heard of him?

PAUL. No.

SHEB. What will the school board do?

PAUL. I don't know but I can guess. Anyway, their
decision will be final.

JANE. Oh.

PAUL (walking to space between CLAIRE and DON).
But at least let's get as much from these
last two meetings as we can. I'd like to
start by asking if you feel these meetings
have changed you in any way. And if so, how?
Claire?

CLAIRE (subdued). Start with someone else.

PAUL. Don?

DON. Yes. I'm different.

PAUL. Better?

DON. I don't know. Different. I guess maybe I'm
the same but at least I'm aware of certain
things about myself . . . so even being
aware that I'm the same, I guess, makes
me different.

ADELE. Can we ask what you learned?

DON. I learned I'm pretty uptight. I'm maybe in-
tolerant of other people. Maybe. (He
rises.) Maybe . . . (He walks to KIM,
almost pleading with her. She doesn't look
at him.) . . . maybe I didn't understand
about other people as much as I should.
(To the others generally.) Maybe it's
my fault--I opened the can of worms that
exploded this whole thing.

KIM. Don't be gallant. It isn't your bag.

DON. I'm not. I mean, if I hadn't told what happened between you and me . . .

KIM. What's the difference? (Looking at him.) If
it didn't come from you, it would have
come from someone else.

DON. But it came from me. I'm sorry about it.

KIM. I'm not. Maybe it made me see . . . (She
stops.)

CLAIRE (rising). It made you face a few truths.
(KIM looks at her, ready to fight.) It
made me face some, too. (To PAUL.) I
don't know if that helps. Sometimes
it's a little difficult to continue living in full
possession of the truth. . . . (She turns away,
moving upstage of PAUL.)

ADELE. It always comes out eventually, Claire.
(CLAIRE turns and looks at ADELE.)

CLAIRE (sighing). I suppose so. (She sits in

chair right of SHEB.) Why is it, no matter
what we do . . . no matter how hard we
try, we make mistakes?

ADELE. Because we're human, Claire. Like most
parents . . . (Looks at BARBARA.) . . . and
teachers.

VICKIE. And kids.

CLAIRE. I think a lot of us find we treat our children
exactly the way our parents treated us. I've
caught myself saying things to my son, things
I hated when my mother said them to me.
It's as though they were on tape and you
just automatically replay them. Sometimes
you simply have to rethink things you always
thought were true.

PAUL. But aren't you doing that? Just by joining
this group?

ADELE. Yes, we are. I knew what Stu Ainsley meant
when he said he'd had a hard day at the office
and what did he need this for? I have a hard
day, too, most days . . . doing really dreary,
uninteresting things . . .

KIM. Up women's lib!

ADELE. But I dragged over here these Thursday
nights because I wanted to know about kids.
I got a lot of surprises.

CLAIRE. So did I. I never dreamed they thought
about half the things they think about.

SHEB. That's funny. I never thought parents
thought about . . . (He amends the sentence.)
I never thought they thought.

CLAIRE (looking at him; half sarcastic). Sweet . . .

DODIE. I think it was a marvelous experience. I
learned a great deal about myself. And I've
absolutely sworn to go on a diet. (Thinking
about that, she takes a small can of peanuts
from her lap and puts them in her purse.)

JERRY. That's a lotta jazz, Dodie. You haven't
          gained a friend or lost a pound. You'll
          be into that can of peanuts the minute
          you get out of here.

DODIE. No!

DON. Why are you putting her down?

JERRY (rising and facing him). 'Cause you're all
          talking about the truth and nobody's telling it.
          What good has this done anybody? You
          found out you got problems, Claire found
          out about her son . . . except she didn't
          really, she knew . . . but now, she has to
          face it every morning. So the ones that
          are left here are no better off and Tony,
          wherever he is, we gotta figure is much
          worse.

PAUL. What did it do for you?

JERRY. Turned me off. I hate to agree with Stu
          Ainsley but the whole program is a crock.

DON. You didn't even try.

JERRY. Why don't you go jog around the room?
          (DON, disgusted, moves to empty chair
          right of VICKIE and sits.)

PAUL. Does anybody here think Jerry has changed?

JERRY. I don't care what they think. (He turns his
          back on the room and walks upstage.)

KIM, VICKIE, DODIE. No . . . he hasn't . . .
          uh uh . . .

DON. He got worse.

JERRY (upstage, back to group). Y'see, they didn't
          like me in the beginning and they still don't
          like me so the whole thing was a waste of
          six weeks.

SHEB. Wrong. We didn't like you before; now we
          hate you.

PAUL. Why?

JERRY (wheeling around, coming downstage left of

DODIE). They resent my intellectual
superiority! (The kids laugh.) Admit it!

SHEB. It's not your intellect, baby. Put it this way.
If you weren't personally a crumb, your
intellect wouldn't bother anyone.

JERRY (walking to PAUL). See? Nobody likes me.
OK. I learned to live with that a long time
ago.

ADELE. Didn't you want to find out why? Isn't
that why you joined this group?

JERRY (facing the group). I knew why. I thought maybe
I could figure out a way to change them.
Not me. Them. I've got as much on the ball
as any kid in this school but they put me
down.

VICKIE. That's not true, Jerry. Why should they?
. . . We?

JERRY. 'Cause no matter how smart I get, to you,
I'm . . . I'm a greaser. 'Cause on my
records in the office, my name isn't Jerry,
it's Geraldo . . . Geraldo Martinez.
'Cause my father wears overalls to work and
gets his hands dirty. OK? 'Cause maybe
I don't have a car . . . or I didn't go to
Miami last spring vacation. But, y'know,
I can't figure it out about the clothes.
Everybody's clothes look crummy. How do
they know my sweat shirts are cheaper
than everybody else's?

JANE. But nobody thinks that way . . .

JERRY. Oh, please don't do the "America the Land
of Opportunity" number. (He turns, sits
on chair DR, facing out.) My father thinks
that. Y'know what made them come here?
'Cause they had two kids that died of one
of those dumb diseases most doctors here
only read about. I was their hope. The

American son. Sure, they got it better.
Indoor plumbing and a TV set. But what
about me? A mother who never came to
a teacher's conference 'cause she's
ashamed she can't speak much English.
I thought if I worked real hard . . . if I
got real smart . . . Yeah! I got all the
opportunities in the world. I'm gonna
make it big. I'm gonna marry the governor's
daughter and get my father-in-law the
Spanish-speaking vote.

CLAIRE.   Are you ashamed of your parents?

JERRY.   No, ma'am. (Firmly.) No, ma'am,
no way! But I can't talk to them. No
more than I can talk to you.

DON.   Try not talking to us. Talk with us.

JERRY.   You don't understand. You're all born
with it.

KIM.   With what?

JERRY.   You start even. I have to work my tail off
to get where you are when you're born.

VICKIE.   If you're born healthy, you start even. We
all mess ourselves up as we go along.

JERRY.   You? Baby, you're on the right side of
town where the good dentists are and the
pin-the-tail-on-the-donkey birthday parties
and the tennis lessons. The whole ball of
wax. And you're even very pretty.

VICKIE.   Maybe. I've got a lot. I know it. My
folks are great. Sometimes it seems like
everybody's got it in for their parents . . .
but that's 'cause you only hear from the
people with problems. When things are OK,
people don't talk about it.

ADELE.   Thank heaven someone's on our side.

VICKIE.   But no matter what you have, Jerry, there's
always someone who has more. And no

matter how pretty you are, there's always
someone prettier. Or someone willing to
. . . to give more than you are. And maybe
there's a boy you like and . . . you lose him.

KIM (surprised). I had you pegged as Miss Security.

VICKIE (putting herself down). Oh, yes. Sometimes,
at a party, I look at the other girls and in
order to stay in the room, I say to myself,
that one's pretty but I have better legs than
she does or my eyes are bigger or I dress
better. Anything. Whatever I can find.

DODIE. Suppose you looked around the room and you
couldn't find anything you had that was better
than anyone else's? (She reaches into her
purse and takes out the peanut can, starts
to open it.)

ADELE. Dodie! (DODIE puts the can away.)

JANE. You go out a lot, don't you?

VICKIE. Some. It's not always the greatest thing
going.

DODIE. It's better than saying you haven't missed
one episode of "All in the Family" (or other
regular television show) all year!

VICKIE. You get in less trouble. . . . (She begins
to cry.)

CLAIRE (going to her). What's the matter?

VICKIE. Nothing.

PAUL. Something you want to share?

VICKIE. It's a little too "here and now."

DON. We've only got one more meeting.

VICKIE. Forget it. (Pulling herself together.) Every
girl goes through it, I guess.

DODIE (wisely). Some boy . . .

CLAIRE. My dear, that's part of growing up.

VICKIE. Please, Claire, don't be motherly.

CLAIRE. Well, if you'd tell us what's upsetting you,
maybe we'd know what to tell you.

VICKIE. I know what you'd tell me. You'd tell me,
　　　"Don't."
CLAIRE. Don't what? (VICKIE looks at her.
　　　CLAIRE realizes what she means.) Well,
　　　maybe we shouldn't go into this. (She
　　　moves to chair right of ADELE and sits.)
ADELE. Are you in love with him?
VICKIE. I thought so. I'm not sure.
PAUL. Maybe it's something we should talk about,
　　　Vickie.
VICKIE. Oh, why? It's all over. We broke up.
SHEB. Maybe you didn't have to break up. If you
　　　really loved . . . the guy.
VICKIE. Maybe he pushed too hard.
SHEB. Well, if a guy and a gal are in love . . . I
　　　mean, well, that's where it's at.
VICKIE. Maybe it is. But you shouldn't have made
　　　it a requirement.
CLAIRE (to ADELE, shocked). Sheb?
SHEB (embarrassed). Why did you have to talk about
　　　it in front of everybody?
VICKIE (bursting out). 'Cause it was on my mind!
DODIE (philosophically, but rather envious). It
　　　certainly is a problem.
KIM. Only because we make it one. If people didn't,
　　　didn't . . .
ACTRESS WHO PLAYS ADELE (interrupting). Excuse
　　　me, but I just don't think we should play
　　　this scene tonight. (To audience.) I'm
　　　sure you'll forgive us if we jump the next two
　　　or three pages. (To the cast.) Take it
　　　from Barbara's entrance.
ACTOR WHO PLAYS PAUL. Now, wait a minute . . .
ACTOR WHO PLAYS JERRY. You can't keep jumping
　　　in and out of the play like this.

(ACTRESS WHO PLAYS BARBARA appears L,

wondering what's going on.)

ACTRESS WHO PLAYS ADELE. We've been doing
it all night, so don't tell me we're losing
the reality of the scene. (To ACTRESS
WHO PLAYS BARBARA.) Let's just go on.
Make your entrance,————. (She uses
Actress Who Plays Barbara's real name.)
ACTRESS WHO PLAYS VICKIE. It's my big scene
and I'm going to play it!
ACTRESS WHO PLAYS ADELE. No! It's too embarrassing. I said so from the first
rehearsal. I see no reason why this play
has to go into . . . romantic entanglements.
ACTOR WHO PLAYS PAUL. Because they are there!
ACTRESS WHO PLAYS ADELE. I know they are
there but they don't have to be here!
ACTOR WHO PLAYS DON. What's biting you?
ACTRESS WHO PLAYS ADELE. I mean you could
upset somebody terribly. (To ACTRESS
WHO PLAYS VICKIE.) You don't care
about people's feelings. You just want to
do the crying scene. (To audience.) I
admit she does it beautifully, but I'm sure
you all understand the point by now, don't
you? (To ACTRESS WHO PLAYS VICKIE.)
Did you ever think that somebody out there
might have had this exact same problem?
ACTRESS WHO PLAYS DODIE. Did you?
ACTOR WHO PLAYS JERRY (startled). Her? She's
a professional choir girl.
ACTRESS WHO PLAYS ADELE. I resent that.
(Grandly.) It just so happens that this same
thing happened to . . . a very close friend
of mine.
ACTRESS WHO PLAYS BARBARA. And she's out
front tonight?

ACTRESS WHO PLAYS ADELE. No. But he is! I
    just don't want to say those words. I'd die.
ACTRESS WHO PLAYS VICKIE. But that's exactly
    the point of this scene. Kids do get into
    hang-ups because they hide the problem.
    They don't talk about it to anybody.
ACTRESS WHO PLAYS ADELE. Who could you tell
    that to?
ACTRESS WHO PLAYS KIM. Your doctor . . . your
    priest . . . for heaven's sake, your mother.
ACTRESS WHO PLAYS ADELE. I couldn't tell my
    mother! (She bursts into tears.) She
    wouldn't listen!
ACTRESS WHO PLAYS DODIE. I was right.
ACTRESS WHO PLAYS JANE (moving to ACTRESS
    WHO PLAYS ADELE and comforting her).
    Now you've made her cry . . .
ACTRESS WHO PLAYS ADELE (weeping and gestur-
    ing out front). In front of him . . .

    (ELAINE appears R with prompt script.)

ELAINE. Where are you now? How do you expect
    me to follow the prompt script?
ACTOR WHO PLAYS PAUL (moving to ACTRESS
    WHO PLAYS ADELE). Look . . . You've
    got to face this. You're not the only one.
    We all have confusions and insecurities . . .
    all of us. . . . We're not children any more
    and like Vickie in the play, we don't know
    how to deal with this. We have grown-up feel-
    ings that they tell us we're not supposed to
    have . . . but they're there . . . and if we
    don't understand them, we have to make
    an effort to face them and talk about them.
ACTOR WHO PLAYS DON. If you can't do that,
    you've really got a problem.

ACTRESS WHO PLAYS ADELE. My mother says
    ladies don't talk about things like that.
    You grow up . . . and . . . and you get
    married . . . and then you find out.
ACTOR WHO PLAYS JERRY. You find out you're
    pretty hung up.
ACTRESS WHO PLAYS ADELE (snapping). I am
    not . . . (Thinks about it, wonders if she
    is, and finishes lamely.) . . . hung up. . . .
ACTRESS WHO PLAYS BARBARA. Problems don't
    go away just because we pretend they aren't
    problems.
ACTRESS WHO PLAYS ADELE. Well, I'm sorry.
    I apologize to everybody . . . (She nods at
    the audience.) . . . but if not wanting to discuss
    . . . sex . . . in front of a theatre full of
    people is a hang-up, I've got it and I won't
    do it. So if you want to finish the play, just
    skip over this scene . . . (Talking to someone
    in audience.) . . . and if you ever mention
    this to anyone, Herbie, I swear I'll . . .
    (Realizing she has revealed his name, she
    begins to cry again. ACTRESS WHO PLAYS
    JANE comforts her.)
ACTOR WHO PLAYS DON. No point arguing. Let's
    go to Barbara's entrance.
ELAINE. I'll never stage manage again as long as I
    live. (She and ACTRESS WHO PLAYS
    BARBARA start off but stop as:)
ACTRESS WHO PLAYS DODIE. Well, I'm going
    to say my line whether she likes it or not.
    'Cause I think it's the best line in the play.
ACTRESS WHO PLAYS ADELE (get it over with).
    Go ahead!
ACTRESS WHO PLAYS DODIE (indicating SHEB).
    I can't unless he says his line first.
ACTRESS WHO PLAYS ADELE (very irritated).

All right! All right! (ELAINE and ACTRESS
WHO PLAYS BARBARA exit. Everyone returns to where they were when the scene
stopped, except PAUL who sits where
Vickie was, and VICKIE and SHEB who
stand together DR.)

SHEB.   I'm sorry, Vickie. I'm sorry I put it the way
I put it. I guess I . . . I feel very strongly
about you . . . and I . . . I . . . I need
reassurance, too. If I say something funny
and people laugh, then I know I'm funny.
But when you say "I love you," you don't
expect a laugh and . . . well, how do you
know?

DODIE.   I always thought if you had someone to say
"I love you" to . . . you said it . . . and
they said the right thing back . . . and you
both just knew what was right for you to do
next.

PAUL.   I've never heard it put better, Dodie.

DODIE (wryly).   I've had a lot of time to think about
it.

(BARBARA enters L, very upset.)

BARBARA.   I'm glad you're all still here. I've just
come from Tony's house. His brother called
me. . . . (She has come down LC. PAUL
moves to her.)

VICKIE.   Is he back?

BARBARA.   No. But they found him.

PAUL.   Where?

BARBARA.   Some little town upstate . . . he was in
his car. . . .

ADELE.   An accident?

BARBARA.   No. Just a simple garden hose from the
exhaust into . . . His brother's gone up

there.

JANE. Is he alive?

BARBARA. Yes . . . but, they're not sure . . .
they're not sure he'll make it. Oh, Paul
. . . I didn't try hard enough! (She falls
against him, he holds her.)

BLACKOUT

Scene 8

(It is before the eighth session. When lights come
        up, PAUL stands alone, lost in thought, UR.
        CLAIRE and ADELE are seated on the bench,
        talking quietly. SHEB and VICKIE are DR
        carrying on a private conversation. DODIE,
        JERRY and JANE are standing DL, also
        talking. KIM sits alone UL. Almost im-
        mediately, BARBARA enters L.)

BARBARA (to KIM). Is Paul here? (KIM gestures to
        PAUL, who, hearing his name, starts
        downstage. BARBARA crosses, meeting
        him C.) I've been trying to get you all day.
PAUL. Did you hear anything? (The others stop
        talking and listen.)
BARBARA. I talked to Tony's brother this morning.
        He brought him home last night.
ADELE. He's all right?
BARBARA. Yes. Fine. (PAUL sighs deeply, very
        relieved.)
CLAIRE. Thank God. (The others murmur similar
        sentiments among themselves.)
PAUL (to BARBARA). Did Tony say anything about
        . . . about the group?
BARBARA. His brother didn't say.
PAUL. Oh.
BARBARA. Have you heard from the school board?
PAUL. They're meeting now. Actually, I'm so
        relieved about Tony, I don't much care what
        they do.
BARBARA. I wish you did care, Paul. This may have
        been a bumpy ride, but I think, eventually,
        we'll see it was worth it.

JANE. Can we start?

PAUL. I suppose so. Everybody want to sit down?

(Those who are standing find seats. PAUL remains
        standing, moves R. DON enters L. KIM
        rises immediately and goes to him.)

KIM. We just heard. Tony's OK.

DON (happy about the news, but not knowing how to
        react to KIM). I'm glad. (He waits a beat,
        begins to move away. She puts a hand on
        his arm, stopping him.)

KIM. Look . . . this is our last meeting.

DON. I know.

KIM (difficult to say this). Y'see . . . I know you
        don't dig pushy girls . . . but, the people
        I stay with are having a party Saturday
        night. . . .

DON (smiling). I'd love to be there.

KIM. This group helped. (Not a put-down; her way
        of saying she likes him.) I think the novo-
        caine in your brain is beginning to wear
        off. (They sit together.)

PAUL. OK?

JANE. Before we start, I just want to say, I don't
        think we should stop. I mean . . . I think

we should continue meeting.

OTHERS. Yes . . . Why don't we? . . . Can we,
          Paul?

PAUL. No. I'm very pleased you want to, but we
        can't.

SHEB. It doesn't matter about the school board. We
        can do it on our own.

JANE. Meet at different people's houses every week
        . . . or even just mine. My folks are in
        Europe anyway.

VICKIE. Couldn't we, Paul?

PAUL. I don't even know that I'll be here. After
        their meeting tonight, I'm pretty sure the
        school board'll cancel the whole program.

DON. But if we're doing it away from school . . .
        by ourselves?

(STU enters L, unnoticed.)

PAUL. I may have to move some place else. I'm
        going to need a job.

STU. I hope not, Paul.

CLAIRE. Stu!

PAUL. What do you mean?

STU (moving to PAUL). I heard about Tony. My
        daughter told me. It was all over the
        school.

JERRY. You better believe it.

STU. I went to see him tonight. We talked for a
        while. Then . . . we went to the school
        board meeting together. He's still there.

PAUL. Oh?

SHEB. Wasn't that putting a knife in a dead horse?

STU. I wanted to retract what I had said. I was
        most anxious. Before they voted on whether
        or not to continue this program.

KIM. What turned you into Santa Claus?

STU. Partly my daughter. Partly Tony. Partly some
changes I feel--in myself.

PAUL. I'm not sure it should be continued. Tony
tried to kill himself. I have to consider
myself responsible.

ADELE. But you mustn't. Maybe Tony shouldn't
have been in this group in the first place.
That is, if he was so disturbed that he
could even think of . . . well, then he needed
more help . . . deeper help than anyone
expects of you.

VICKIE. She's right. This was supposed to be a
group for fairly normal people with usual
problems.

KIM. Only the half-crazies.

PAUL. Nevertheless I set him off.

STU. Maybe you did. Maybe I did. He might have
done it without anybody interfering. The
point is, you're trying. That's what I
told them . . . the board. It's an experi-
ment but it stands a chance of being a
help. I said I hoped it would continue.
Because, for one thing, I'd like my daughter
in the next group.

PAUL (surprised). Well, I . . .

STU. I used to think . . . isn't it stupid? . . . I
thought I was the only father who couldn't
. . . well, get through to his child. That
mine was the special case. But I found out
here, she's really no worse than the other
kids . . . and none of them are so bad
when you really look.

SHEB. Isn't that funny? Y'know, I used to hate
authority figures--parents . . . teachers
. . . (Surprised.) Some of you are cool!

PAUL. I don't know. . . . I'd really like some
time to think this all out. If I started

fresh, somewhere else, maybe I could do
better. I don't mean I'm not glad we did
this. I am. I hope it's been productive for
you.

DODIE. Oh, yes . . . yes, it was.

JANE. Couldn't we continue if we all chipped in?

(TONY enters L. ACTOR WHO PLAYS TONY is
still upset and it must show through in
the few lines he speaks in character, but
the audience should not be sure whether
this tension is in the actor or the character.)

TONY. Mr. Tobin. . . .

PAUL (going to him). Tony, I'm so sorry. . . .

TONY. No. Don't be. It wasn't you. If I was smart
enough to take advantage of what you tried
. . . I told them that . . . it helped. . . .
Before that . . . no one . . . no one . . .
(He can't seem to remember.)

ACTOR WHO PLAYS PAUL (trying to stay in
character and still help the actor). Yes,
Tony . . . what are you trying to say?

TONY. That . . . that . . .

ACTOR WHO PLAYS PAUL. Just take it easy, Tony
. . . get a grip on yourself . . .

TONY. Before that no one . . . (He breaks out of
character.) I'm sorry. I can't. . . . I
thought I could get through this scene but
I . . .

ACTRESS WHO PLAYS BARBARA (moving to him,
comforting him). It doesn't matter.

ACTOR WHO PLAYS JERRY. Yes, it does! This is
getting to be embarrassing!

ACTRESS WHO PLAYS JANE. Can we please get on
with the play?

ACTOR WHO PLAYS TONY. No! I have to explain.

I shouldn't have said what I said before.
Y'see . . . my father's here tonight . . .
or he's supposed to be . . . and I want him
to understand. (Moving to ACTOR WHO
PLAYS STU.) Y'see, when you started
off the stage before . . . when you wouldn't
take the time to listen to me . . . well . . .
it was like you were him. My father.
Actually. It suddenly seemed so real.
Like I've been there. Like . . . I've never
felt close to my father. Almost maybe
like I wasn't important enough for him to
bother with. And that's maybe why I'm
shy with other people. Maybe it's why I
like being in plays so I can be somebody
else. But in this play . . . I . . . I
turned out to be me all over again. That's
why I was so against this play, I guess.

ACTRESS WHO PLAYS ADELE. This play was too
much. My mother said it all along.

ACTOR WHO PLAYS TONY. But while I was back-
stage . . . and the play was going on . . .
I kept wondering why I blew up . . . like
I couldn't figure why that moment got to me
like that. And then suddenly--(To ACTOR
WHO PLAYS STU.)--I saw you couldn't
listen to me because of your own hang-ups.
I mean the character's hang-ups.

ACTOR WHO PLAYS JERRY (angry). All right.
You've explained.

ACTOR WHO PLAYS TONY. Not quite. . . .

ACTOR WHO PLAYS JERRY. For Pete's sake,
_____ . 　　　(Uses his real name.)
We're in the middle of a play. All this
stopping and starting . . . you're making
fools of us!

ACTOR WHO PLAYS TONY (getting angry, too).

You don't want to listen, either. You're
thinking about how you look!

ACTOR WHO PLAYS JERRY. Why not?

ACTOR WHO PLAYS TONY. That's the whole
point! I was thinking just about me. What
I never thought about before tonight was,
what about him? My dad! He looks like
he's got everything he wants. The money.
The business. I mean, when you need
something you go to your dad. Right?
I know things worry me . . . frighten
me . . . But I never thought, maybe he's
scared, too. Maybe there are outside
things that bother him that have nothing
to do with me. Maybe he worries that
when I need something, maybe he won't
have it to give me. He's really . . . some
of you know him . . . he's really a good
guy. I'm sorry I interrupted again, but
. . . I had to explain so people wouldn't
think . . . I mean . . . he's a good guy
. . . (Drained, he sits far L.)

ACTRESS WHO PLAYS KIM (going to him). But
that's why we were right to do this play.

ACTOR WHO PLAYS JERRY. We haven't done it
yet. I don't think we ever will!

ACTRESS WHO PLAYS BARBARA. Shut up!

ACTRESS WHO PLAYS JANE. He's right!

ACTRESS WHO PLAYS KIM (to ACTOR WHO PLAYS
TONY). Maybe it upset you . . . but it
had something to say and you learned
from it.

ACTRESS WHO PLAYS JANE (coming downstage).
I've listened five weeks and I don't
know what it has to say!

ACTOR WHO PLAYS JERRY (to her). Don't you
start now!

ACTRESS WHO PLAYS KIM (to ACTRESS WHO
      PLAYS JANE). Look, I'm not into drugs.
      I hate the idea. I get all the kicks I
      need being in a play . . . making ceramics
      . . . doing things! I never understood why
      kids get into drugs until I began to wonder
      how to act Kim. So I looked around. And
      when I really looked, I understood. They're
      insecure . . . or frightened. They think
      they can get high and float right over a
      bad situation. But they can't. They come
      right back down in the middle of it . . .
      but now they've made it worse.
ACTOR WHO PLAYS DON. If they just realized
      everyone has problems . . . and pretty much
      the same ones.
ACTRESS WHO PLAYS JANE. What good would
      that do?
ACTOR WHO PLAYS JERRY (to ACTRESS WHO
      PLAYS JANE). Will you come on,_____ .
      (He uses her real name.)
ACTRESS WHO PLAYS JANE. Wait a minute. I'm
      interested now!
ACTRESS WHO PLAYS DODIE (rising and going
      to her). A lot of good. It's not nice to feel
      alone. I've never been in a play before.
      I was always embarrassed by how I look.
      When they asked me to play Dodie I knew
      why. Remember, I said "no" at first?
      Because I was insulted. Then I said to
      myself, what have you got to be insulted
      about? They want a fat girl, you're fat!
      OK. Maybe that makes me closer to my
      part than the rest of you are to yours. But
      at least, now I feel there are other fat
      girls . . . somewhere . . . who say "I
      had nowhere else to go so I came to a

group meeting." I had nowhere else to go
so I came to rehearsals. (She is upset.
She walks to the proscenium R, faced
away from the others.) Y'know something
else? Dodie says nobody ever kissed her.
Maybe I did this whole thing so I could do
the scene where _____ (She uses
Actor who Plays Don's real name) kissed
me. (She throws a chocolate bar in her hand
to the floor, leans against the proscenium
almost crying, then pulls herself together.)
Y'know something else? I lost four pounds
during rehearsals.

ACTOR WHO PLAYS SHEB (moving to her, talking
to her though she remains faced away).
I feel the same way,_____ .
(He uses her real name.)

ACTRESS WHO PLAYS DODIE. No.

ACTOR WHO PLAYS SHEB. You're trapped inside
the fat girl. I'm hung with the class clown.
That's why I got my part. Inside, there's
really a very nice, serious guy trying to
get out. Only he's afraid without the jokes
. . . the bits . . . that nobody would pay
any attention to him.

ACTRESS WHO PLAYS DODIE (turning to him,
surprised). Do you feel that way, too?

ACTOR WHO PLAYS SHEB (nodding). And, anyway,
you're not that fat!

(ELAINE comes on R, pointing to audience.)

ELAINE. Those people out there did not pay for
an evening of group therapy.

ACTRESS WHO PLAYS KIM. At what these tickets
cost, it's cheaper than the real thing.

ACTOR WHO PLAYS JERRY. It turned out to be the

real thing.

ELAINE. It's a play. Just a play. It sets up a
situation . . . has a couple of sad scenes
. . . a couple of jokes . . . makes a
little point about human relations . . .
and we all go home. Let's go.

ACTRESS WHO PLAYS JANE. I don't think it makes
any point. I can't identify with Jane. I think
Jane is an idiot.

ACTRESS WHO PLAYS VICKIE. Then you should
identify easily.

ACTRESS WHO PLAYS JANE. She's shy. Mr.
Harris says because she's insecure.
Well . . . everybody's insecure one way
or another. I'm insecure. I threw up every
morning during mid-terms.

ACTOR WHO PLAYS STU. Well, doesn't that prove
the point?

ACTRESS WHO PLAYS JANE. What point? Vickie
doesn't know whether it's wrong to make
it with Sheb. Don doesn't know how to
handle a relationship with a girl. Kim's
into drugs . . . (Pointing to DODIE and
SHEB.) She's fat, he's funny. What's different? We all know a hundred people
like that.

ELAINE. Look, the whole thing is summed up in
Tony's speech. Do your speech, Tony.

ACTOR WHO PLAYS TONY (very tight). No . . .
I can't . . .

ACTRESS WHO PLAYS BARBARA. Please. . . .

ACTOR WHO PLAYS JERRY. Oh, come on,
_____.(Uses his real name.) We'll
never get out of here!

ACTOR WHO PLAYS TONY (flaring). Get off my
back! I can't do it! That whole thing with
the circle again . . . I can't . . . it's

too real to me.

ACTRESS WHO PLAYS JANE. It's only another
page. Why don't we forget the whole
thing and go to the party?

ACTRESS WHO PLAYS BARBARA (to ACTOR WHO
PLAYS TONY). You can't just quit! (He
remains silent, head in hands.) If working
on this play has taught us anything, it's
that we're not alone. Maybe this play
bothers some of the rest of us . . .

ACTOR WHO PLAYS JERRY (to ELAINE). Read
the speech for him, Elaine.

ELAINE. That'll look silly.

ACTRESS WHO PLAYS JANE. You think it looks
sensible now? Read!

ACTRESS WHO PLAYS BARBARA (to ACTOR WHO
PLAYS TONY, using his real name).
_____ ,it's more important for you than
for the play for you to do this. (All look at
him. He remains silent.)

ELAINE (opening playbook she carries; to audience).
This is where he's telling them what he
told the school board. (The others resume
positions they were in when scene stopped.
BARBARA moves last, reluctantly.) I told
them that . . . that it wasn't Mr. Ainsley's
fault that he walked out on the group. I
realized after he left that he was just worried
. . . in his way . . . about his kid. I . . .
I didn't want to make it look as though you
were wrong, Mr. Ainsley.

STU. But I was. (ACTOR WHO PLAYS TONY looks
up, begins to watch.)

ELAINE (as TONY). Only you shouldn't have been
worrying just about your kid . . . you
should've been worrying about all the
kids. Like they should worry about everybody,

       too. It sounds like a lot, I know . . . but
       if everybody understands we're all in this
       together . . . then none of it is really so
       bad, is it?

JANE. What do you think the school board will do?
       (ACTOR WHO PLAYS TONY rises.)

ELAINE and ACTOR WHO PLAYS TONY(together).
       I don't know, but . . . (ELAINE stops,
       looks at ACTOR WHO PLAYS TONY. He
       continues alone.)

TONY. I think there's a chance they'll let it continue.

BARBARA. Oh, Paul, that's wonderful!

PAUL. Why do you think that? (TONY moves to
       ELAINE's place. She blends to DR and
       watches.)

TONY. I don't know. . . . Just the way they looked.
       I told them I was never really "in" before.
       . . .

PAUL. You have to break in!

TONY. Break into what?

PAUL (to others). Form the circle--quickly! (They
       are forming circle.)

TONY. I'd like to be in . . . in for good.

PAUL. Then do it!

TONY. I can't!

PAUL. It's up to you.

BARBARA. Tony, try! (He shakes his head. She
       screams his real name.)＿＿. You must!
       (He crashes against the circle, trying to
       break in.)

PAUL. Don't make it easy . . . hold on . . .
       make him earn it. . . .

VICKIE and BARBARA. Go ahead . . . break in.
       . . . Go on! (Finally he breaks in.)

TONY (in center of circle). I did . . . I did . . .
       (He is shaking, happy. BARBARA comforts
       him. They break the circle.)

ACTRESS WHO PLAYS JANE (coming downstage,
        a light breaking). Oh, I see! I see what the
        play's about!
ACTOR WHO PLAYS SHEB (to ELAINE, who has been
        watching, fascinated). Elaine! The curtain!
        (She dashes off R.)
ACTRESS WHO PLAYS JANE. It's part of growing
        up . . . and no matter how old you are, you
        never really stop.
ACTRESS WHO PLAYS VICKIE. I almost feel as
        though this isn't a play . . . that these
        people aren't really made-up characters.
        Maybe . . . (To ACTOR WHO PLAYS
        PAUL.) . . . maybe these people are
        really us. . . .
ACTOR WHO PLAYS PAUL (looking at the audience).
        Or them.

                        CURTAIN

PRODUCTION NOTES

COSTUMES:

As Harris says in Scene One, wear pretty much the clothes you would normally wear to an extra-curricular meeting or rehearsal. The only exceptions are:

> The ACTRESS WHO PLAYS KIM should wear fairly attractive rehearsal clothes in the first three scenes to dramatize extremely far-out, scruffy look as Kim in scenes 4 and 5. In Scene 6, as Kim she should wear a dress to show Kim's emergence from her rebellious attitude.

> Rehearsal clothes for ACTOR WHO PLAYS JERRY might be a little better than average to show difference when he wears poorer clothes as Jerry from Scene 4 on.

As each scene in the play and in the play within the play are supposed to take place a week apart, there should be some change of clothing. Wonders can be done with adding or removing jackets or sweaters if plain, dark, nondescript slacks and skirts are worn. For the boys, , slip-on knit shirts can be changed rapidly. That will be about as much as there will be time for after Scenes 1 and 2. Those who make late entrances in Scene 4 might have a chance for a complete change. If possible it is especially important for those playing adults (Stu, Barbara, Claire, Adele and Paul) to change here .

Between Scenes 4 and 5 there is little time for anything but jacket changes. After Scene 5 everyone can make a c o m p l e t e change. From Scene 5 on, Elaine need not change at all. For Scene 7, only Barbara would have time for a complete change. All of these quick "jacket" changes should be made in the wings for the sake of speed. Clothes can, of course, be repeated. As nice as it would be to have the changes, if they become a time problem, it is far better to keep the play going and forget about changing clothes.

TO THE DIRECTOR:

I have included several floor plans, more for clarity in reading than direction, necessarily, although I feel they work. If you wish to do other blocking, feel free to do so. An interesting effect might be achieved by having rapping students sitting on the floor, and those joining a discussion leaving their chairs to join them. Adults could remain on chairs, establishing a certain gap between the groups. Sitting on the floor will work, however, only if your sight lines permit.

A WORD TO THE ACTORS:

I believe this will be a fascinating play to perform because, in effect, each of the actors plays two parts: the character in "Here and Now" and the character of the actor playing that part. Although I have requested this c h a r a c t e r be called by the actor's own name, it will help to think of this as a characterization, however close to your own personality. Some of the "actor" parts (notably Sheb and Dodie) are very close to the play parts. The others, especially Jane, Jerry and the adult c h a r a c t e r s, should make e v e r y effort to differentiate between "actor" and "part." The play requires tremendous concentration for the actors. At the beginning they must believe the theatre is empty. They must play the various scenes when the actors come out of the play as truthfully as possible . . . confuse the audience, if you can, as to what is a rehearsed play and what is ad lib truth. To aid this, I have already suggested a line saying "No Intermission" in the program. If you can make your audience really believe you had to stop the performance, the play can have a tremendous effect. For the same reason, it would be exciting if the director and stage managers appeared as themselves.

This is a play where listening is even more important than usual. Almost everyone is on stage continuously due to the nature of the situation in the play. Each part has its own big moments and the reaction, response and attention each actor gives to the other's big scene will only improve the performance of his own.

Learn the lines you are supposed to be reading. If you actually rely on the book in your hand, you are bound to lose your place and destroy the reality and pace of the scene. Play the catching sequence in Scene 2 very rapidly: once that action begins the dialogue is not that important and I would prefer talking over each other's lines to deadly pauses. Talking over Tony's lines will be very important at the end of Scene 5. Rehearse both sequences carefully.

I cannot emphasize strongly enough the necessity of playing this as truthfully and as real-ly as you can. If you make the audience believe in both your characters, it will be a very powerful evening in the theatre.

PROPERTIES

GENERAL: Chairs, stool, piano bench.

ELAINE: Chair, pencil or pen, piece of paper with announcement written on it, prompt script or playbook, flashlight (Scene 4).

MARVIN: Small table, script, flashlight (if needed for Scene 5).

STU: Cigarettes.

JERRY: Pencil.

DON: Cast on hand, which later is changed to sling and bandage.

DODIE: Chocolate bar, box of caramel corn, lollypop, large half-eaten chocolate bar, small can of peanuts, another chocolate bar.

HARRIS: Briefcase containing playbooks and a notebook, flashlight (if needed for Scene 5), clipboard.

PAUL: Stop watch.

Note: In Scene 2, all except Adele, Jerry and Kim carry playbooks. From Scene 3, only the stage managers have scripts. Girls may carry purses.

DIRECTOR'S NOTES

DIRECTOR'S NOTES

DIRECTOR'S NOTES

ACN- 8907

DIRECTOR'S NOTES

PS
3568
O43
H4
1973

0 00 02 0575917 8
MIDDLEBURY COLLEGE